Fifty-Five Years on the Bench

Richard W. Varichak

To: Tasha, Nick & family:

I'm Happy to present you with a copy of my book, "55 YEARS ON THE BENCH," to celebrate your addition to our MESABI DRIVE and becoming a very special next door NEIGHBOR.

I believe you will enjoy the book because of its positive and FRIENDLY approach to the coaching WORLD. IT WAS TRULY a labor of LOVE for me and proved to be an exciting and fulfilling experience. So, I hope you will find the book both entertaining and worthwhile!

— Coach DICK VARICHAK

Fifty-Five Years on the Bench

Published by V.L. Jacobson & Company, Inc.
920 East 21st Street
Hibbing, MN 55746

Copyright © 2013 by Richard W. Varichak
All rights reserved, including the right to reproduce
this book or portions thereof in any form whatsoever.

ISBN 978-1-4675-6404-5

For information, address V.L. Jacobson & Company, Inc.,
920 East 21st Street, Hibbing, MN 55746.

Paperback edition printed January, 2013
Express Print One, Ltd., Hibbing, MN 55746
Cover design by Renee A. Anderson

Acknowledgments

As mentioned previously in my tipoff introduction, the idea of recording my numerous coaching experiences was instigated by Paul McLaughlin, one of our very active basketball parents. His interest in my coaching life was flattering and the suggestion that I reveal those moments in print gave life to "Fifty-Five Years on the Bench." I thank Paul for his interest and for moving me to more literary efforts.

I can't thank the hundreds of former student athletes enough who answered my call for their input in putting this book together. The response to my invitations was heart-warming and I didn't realize that so many former athletes were eager to divulge their memories of Coach V. and his place in their lives.

Thanks also to the parents who contributed, not only their offspring and many of my memorable coaching moments, but who added segments of their own to the book, which I greatly appreciated. Also, to those considerate mothers and fathers who never let me pay for my coffee from the concession stand. You made me feel important! Thank you.

I'm truly indebted to Mark Stodgill and Rick Weegum of the Duluth News Tribune, Ted Anderson of the Hibbing Daily Tribune, and Mary Keyes, proprietor of the Howard Book Store in Hibbing, for their time and helpful suggestions after reading the rough draft.

Finally, to the most important part of this venture, my family, who not only took the time to help put this publication together, but gave me loads of support. Eternal thanks to my grand-daughter, Lindsay, for deciphering my printed words and making them readable through their time consuming typing of the rough draft. To Vikki, for the hours she invested editing and formatting the many drafts of my work, bringing it to publication. And to Noka, the love of my life, for her unquestioned loyalty to all my efforts in trying to mold my athletes to be better players and more important, better citizens.

- Coach V.

Table of Contents

Dedication 7
Forward by Doug Schmitz 6
Tip-Off 9
Chapter 1: The Far East - Coaching Interest Starts Early 11
Chapter 2: Military Athletes - The Chosen Few 15
Chapter 3: Coaching Idols Who Brought Me into the Fold 19
Chapter 4: Male and Female Athletes Play on Different Planes 27
Chapter 5: Evant Elks 35
Chapter 6: Doug Schmitz - A Study in Perfection Required 41
Chapter 7: Hibbing Cardinal Cager - Basketball Can Be So Much Fun .. 59
Chapter 8: Athletes Can Produce the Wierdest Sitcoms 71
Chapter 9: Nine Talented Ladies - They Turned the Program Around .. 79
Chapter 10: My Senior Citizens - They Came to Play 87
Chapter 11: The Highs and Lows of Coaching 89
Chapter 12: You Have to be an Amateur Psychologist to Coach 95
Chapter 13: The Players Who Made My Job an Adventure 101
Chapter 14: Assistant Coaches - A Blessing on the Side 111
Chapter 15: Junior College Football Was Fun 119
Chapter 16: Would You Coach a Relative? 131
Chapter 17: My Solid Six 151
Chapter 18: Basketball Summer Camps - Are They Worth It? 157
Chapter 19: Parents Can Be Fun 165
Chapter 20: Student Team Managers Run the Show 179
Chapter 21: The Last Hurrah! 193
Final Buzzer 193

Dedication

As I sit down to record the many pleasant experiences contained in this book, I want to emphasize that the objective sought in the writing is basically a labor of love. There isn't any desire to make this a best seller, money-maker or a guide to better coaching. It's been enjoyable for me to relive the past 55 years and especially to read the many enlightening contributions sent in by my former student athletes.

So, to all the wonderful players who made my coaching world a happy and fulfilling adventure, I dedicate, to you, this labor of love. My ever-lasting gratitude also goes out to my loving family and very helpful parents and grandparents who made my job a worthwhile and exciting profession.

Figure 1 The Varichak Family - November 2012
L to R: Vikki, Pam, Dick, Tom, Noka, and Donny.

Fifty-Five Years on the Bench

Forward

There is a saying: "The most valuable thing that you can give someone is your time." I could never come close to repaying Dick Varichak for all the time he spent helping me run a basketball program. Coach V was very generous in all things, and especially his time. How fortunate could I be to have a person become your assistant coach who was a head high school coach and college coach, let alone my own college coach. Coach V was very much a "players' coach" as he always had the players' best interests at heart for over 50 years.

I met Coach Varichak in June of 1972 at Hibbing Community College when I was working for his dad, George, during a summery work study job. George recommended me to his son, Dick, the head basketball coach, at HCC, and gave me a basketball to shoot with during my lunch break. Dick was a major influence for me to enter into coaching. I am now in my 37th year, assisting at Mountain Iron-Buhl High School with the girls' basketball program after coaching both high school and college students.

I played both basketball and baseball for Coach V at HCC for 2 years. Together, we turned the HCC baseball program from a club sport to a college team. Once Dick retired from the college, he became my assistant for 18 more years. After approximately 1500 practices and 500 games together in the gym, I still can't say thank you enough for everything he has done for me and for all the great times we had together. I can't even count the number of times he supervised open gyms or went along on scouting trips.

Coach Dick Varichak is fully retired from his coaching duries now, but he still attends many games. Coach V was my coach, and I coached his son, and we both coached my daughter and his granddaughter at Hibbing High School. Now I am coaching with Jeff Buffetta at MIB High School, who I coached in college. Dick Varichak's influence? Yes! For everyone he coached, our lives are much richer because of him. Enjoy his basketball treasure trove of stories!

Forward: Tip-Off

Tip-Off

    A reader who investigates the content of this book would probably feel they will be following numerous legal and court room battles because of the title. Actually, all the action takes place on the sidelines of football fields, gymnasiums, baseball diamonds, tennis courts, and golf courses.

    On my wedding day in Corpus Christi, Texas, on June 15, 1955, I had to report back to my Navy base at Kingsville to play in a baseball doubleheader. Since that wedding date, my wife, and later on my children, have been introduced to a multitude of athletic facilities in the pursuit of my profession as a teacher and coach. My coaching tenure actually began two years before my marriage, serving Navy tours in Yokosuka, Japan in 1953 and Moffet Field, California in 1954.

    For the next 53 consecutive years, I found myself directing a variety of athletic squads, both male and female. So, when did I decide to write this book? I believe the seed was planted by one of our basketball parents, Mr. Paul McLaughlin. Paul and I were discussing basketball in the gym at Thief River Falls, just prior to our Bluejacket-Thief River Falls varsity game. I mentioned to Paul that I had one of the most weird and strange experiences here in this gym when I brought one of my Hibbing Junior College Cardinals cagers to face Northland Community College. As I described the incident, which I will cover in its entirety in a later chapter, Paul remarked to me, "Dick, why don't you put all these experiences down in a book. I have listened to your stories the past couple years and you never repeat yourself." I found this idea challenging and exciting and thus <u>Fifty-Five Years on The Bench</u> was born.

    I wanted memory input from my former players, so my next project was to locate many of these student athletes. The response to my request was very positive. Some of my former athletes are now grandfathers and grandmothers and were in their middle sixties. What a thrill!

    I discovered many aspects of my coaching career from these letters. If I didn't know it before, I came to realize that I chose the profes-

Fifty-Five Years on the Bench

sion that gave me the greatest feeling of accomplishment and fulfillment. I hope this book can help motivate deserving young men and women to undertake the thrilling and exciting profession of coaching.

The content of this book is based solely on my feelings and experiences and reflects the philosophy of only one coach. It is not a bible for beginning coaching but may serve as more of an informational tool.

R.W.V

Chapter 1: The Far East - Coaching Interest Starts Early

At my first duty station, after 11 weeks of recruit training, the U.S. Navy shipped me to Yokosuka, Japan to serve with the Commander Naval Forces, Far East. It didn't take long for the Athletic Department on the base to discover my participation in inter-collegiate athletics at the University of Minnesota-Duluth and Hibbing Junior College before entering the Navy. I was recruited to play both basketball and fast pitch softball for the base teams, and received my first coaching contract in 1953 to direct the softball team. I had some second thoughts when Lieutenant Karl Reed, the Athletic Officer, offered me the position. I would be coaching players twice my age, commissioned officers, and teammates with lots of talent.

I had played in the summer 1952 with the Headquarters Support Activity team, a division of the main base team. We were very successful, winning 25 and losing 7, and ended up as Division Champions. When I moved over to the base team as player-coach the next summer, I took several members of our Headquarters team with me. They included my basketball teammates, Don McQuillan, Gayle Morrison, Bill Washer, and Elmer Lindquist. McQuillan was an outstanding pitcher who had a blazing fast ball, along with an assortment of other pitches. Morrison was hustling second sacker, who worked many double play situations with me at shortstop. Lindquist was a heavy hitting outfielder while Washer cleaned up everything that came his way at first base. I also inherited a couple of officers, who contributed important roles in our 38-7 season record. Ensign Clyde McCampbell and Lieutenant Commander Chuck Young, our Base communications Officer, couldn't make every game because of their military duties, but were instrumental in our team's play when they were in the lineup.

Team practice, at times, was an exercise in creativity for me-sometimes we had a full team; other times only a few players- because

Fifty-Five Years on the Bench

duty commitments took precedence over athletic events. Most of my team members were good athletes and did not need a lot of guidance and direction. Military rank was dropped during the season, although the enlisted personnel and the commissioned officers did not socialize with each other.

At the start of the season I discussed the batting order, sub patterns and coaching signals with the team. I felt, at my young age, I didn't know everything and wanted to pick the brains of our older, more experienced players. I received good input from the players and I believe this helped immensely with my coaching decisions. The biggest opposition to some of my decisions came when I had to make changes and substitutions. Mainly it was the younger players who didn't want to come out of the game. This didn't prove to be a big problem but it was the only negative aspect of my first coaching experience.

Goodbye Japan- hello California! I received my transfer orders from Japan in November 1953 and was back home in Chisholm on December 7th. Oh! What a great feeling to be home again after a two year absence from my loved ones. I fully expected to be assigned to a ship in my next duty station, but was pleasantly surprised when the Navy sent me to the Naval Air Station, Moffet Field in California. The base was only a few miles from San Jose and just south of San Francisco.

Once again, just two days after reporting for duty, I was approached by my Commanding Officer who coached a city team basketball squad, in Mt. View, a small town a few dribbles away from the base. He was being transferred and wanted me to take over the team to play and serve as the player-coach. Naturally this interested me and I was quick to jump into the coaching picture again.

I found out the popular saying "You must have thoroughbreds to win the Kentucky Derby" when I began my player-coach tenure with the Mt. View five. Where I was surrounded by top-notch players with the Yokosuka Seahawks, I discovered my personnel at Mt. View had a hard time performing the simplest skill tasks and thus our won-loss record was fairly dismal, although I believe most of the players enjoyed the games. I learned the basic lesson in Coaching 101 that a coach will be a winner as

Richard W. Varichak

long as they have "thoroughbreds" playing for them. Whereas I spent little time in conducting skill drills with the Seahawks, much of my coaching time was involved with teaching my Mt. View cagers the basics on how to play basketball. It was satisfying and I enjoyed the experience, but it showed me that the field of coaching involved more than x's and o's.

Figure 2: Photo by Dick Varichak
Yokosuka Naval Base (Japan) – 1953 NATIONAL TOURNEY RUNNER-UPS
Back row (standing): Josh Miller, Allen Frame, Gayle Morrison, Todd Jones, Don McQuillan, Barry Avers.
Kneeling Row: Chuck Young, Don Pleasant, Jerry Cook, Clyde McCampbell, Elmer Lindquist, Brett Hurd, Terry Capers.
Front: Bill Washer

Chapter 2: Military Athletes - The Chosen Few

The U.S. Military has always provided an athletic outlet for their enlistees, draftees, and career service personnel. No matter where military installations were located, the athlete always had a chance of being selected to play for the base team. The larger the base the more opportunity there was to snatch the top-notch players, usually from the top college programs or from the professional ranks.

I had the opportunity to go through this selection process and played service ball at all three military bases to which I was assigned. Not being a super athlete, I had the opportunity to play with the Yokosuka Seahawks, a big base team with Division I athletes, then on to a less athletic city team in Mt. View, California and finally to a medium size base and athletic program at NAAS Kingsville, Texas in 1955. I had the pleasure to serve as a player-coach at all three bases and felt that military competition made me a better player and further motivated me to be a professional coach.

Figure 3 Photo by U.S. Navy - Sendai, Japan
Dick Varichak is presented the Most Valuable Player trophy by his Coach, Hank Chapman, at the conclusion of the 1952 National Service Basketball Tourney in Sendai, Japan.

As soon as personnel were assigned to the Yokosuka, Japan base, coaches pored through the service records for athletic talent. I was selected shortly after reporting for duty and spent the two years with the base basketball and fast pitch softball teams. Some of my teammates included Don McQuillan from Kansas State, Elmer Lindquist from Detroit University, Bill Washer of Akron University,

Fifty-Five Years on the Bench

Curtis Smith a North Texas University grad, and Clyde McCampbell of Tennessee State, to name a few talented athletes.

When our base football team faced the Army 40th AAA gridders from Tokyo in the Rice Bowl on January 1, 1953, they had the misfortune to knock heads with the army's Arnold Galiffa and Barney Poole from West Point, Clayton Tonnemaker, All-American linebacker from the University of Minnesota and Green Bay Packers, along with Jack Stroud, All-American tackle from Tennessee University and the New York Giants of the NFL. Needless to say, our Navy team got clobbered 66-6 and was never in the game. Galiffa completed 17 passes, good for four touchdowns. Tonnemaker was in our backfield all afternoon and Stroud opened up massive holes in over-matched defensive line. 40th AAA was an Army processing base where military personnel were assigned on their way to Korea and the war-or as our politicians referred to it, a "peace keeping conflict."

As a member of the Seahawk basketball team, we were fortunate to win in our part of the world and were scheduled to compete in Hawaii in the All-Pacific playoffs. Our opponent was San Diego Naval Station led by George Yardly, a 6'9" former Stanford All-American scoring machine. He was a reserve officer who had been called back to active duty while performing with the Golden State Warrior professional basketball team. Although we played San Diego close we couldn't stop Yardly as he torched us for 69 points in their 98-87 win.

I remember watching Big Ten football during World War Two from 1941 to 1945. Once again, athletes were recruited by various military bases and the one familiar to Minnesotans was Iowa Navy Pre-Flight out of Iowa City. Former Gopher players, Bill Daley, a Big Ten All-Conference star and Herman Frickey, who performed as a running back at 155 pounds, entered the Marines Corps and played for the Pre-Flighters for two years. They came back to Minneapolis to help the Iowa Service team upset the Gophers 13-7. Also starring for the Navy team was Otto Graham, a quarterback from Northwestern University and later a star for the professional Cleveland Browns. Iowa Pre-Flight, with their

Richard W. Varichak

multitude of Division I and pro players, played a Division I schedule until the war ended and the base closed.

Morale was very important in the military and the opportunity to engage in competitive sports made service life a memorable and exciting experience.

Figure 4: Photo by U.S. Navy - Yokosuka, Japan
1952 NATIONAL SERVICE BASKETBALL CHAMPIONS
1st Row: Dick Varichak, Bill Washer, Val Bielecki, Gayle Morrison, Jack Bonsall.
2nd Row: Don Hamilton, Bob Webb, Elmer Lindquist, Allen Frame, William Volkert.

Chapter 3: Coaching Idols Who Brought Me into the Fold

My first actual coaching experience came about when I turned fourteen years of age. As a member of the Roosevelt playground softball team in the Chisholm Recreational Department, I was asked to direct the Roosevelt midgets by Recreation Director Swede Pergol. This also gave me the opportunity to coach my younger brother Kenny, who was a pretty good infielder. Swede was my American Legion Coach and one of the finest baseball technicians I was ever to encounter. He placed me on the team as a 7th grader, the youngest player on the squad. I could hit, run, and field, but he filled me in on the strategy of playing the game. He taught me how to get a jump on the ball when fielding, steal a base, when to throw to certain bases, and showed me how to be disciplined at the plate. His easygoing personality and patience in his coaching methods gave me my first building block in establishing a coaching and teaching philosophy.

Early in my elementary years (3rd grade), we started playing competitive basketball and our coach at Roosevelt was Chisholm High School Bluestreak player Ed Tekautz. Ed was 6 '3" and served as one of Coach Harvey J. Roels' centers on the varsity squad. I was starting to grow and was by far the tallest player on the team. Coach Tekautz latched on to me right away and I was quickly learning how to play a low post type of game. Ironically, although I did not play a low post during my varsity career, I was able to use these low post moves in my play as a forward when I played with the varsity. Many thanks Ed!

Of course, one of the most important teachers in my formative training was Coach Roels, my high school basketball and track coach. He thrilled me by elevating my play to varsity basketball competition while I was a freshman. Although I didn't get to play a great many minutes, I learned a ton of coaching strategy sitting next to the head man. I watched

Fifty-Five Years on the Bench

Coach Harvey J. Roels

Figure 5: Photo fom CHS 1948 Yearbook
Coach Harvey J. Roels

A graduate of Lawrence College in Wisconsin, Coach Roels came to CHS in 1922. His credentials were already imposing: he had coached state high school basketball champions in Appleton, Wisconsin in 1918, and in Ishpeming, Michigan in 1920. By 1934 he would complete his triangle of Lake Superior states' cage titles when his Chisholm team won the Minnesota crown.

For 33 years, until he retired from his coaching duties in 1954, Roels worked first to establish and then to sustain the tremendous reputation of the Blue Streaks on the hardwoods of the state. Besides the state crown, his teams won 11 District 28 titels and six Region 7 crowns.

After 1954, Roels served as athletic director and physical education instructor until his retirement. He died in 1967 at the age of 74.

From: History of CHS Sports by
Larry Belluzzo

him make moves on the bench that resulted in many wins for us, and even if we were on the losing end the strategy invoked proved to be extremely useful.

I cite one of his strategic moves as very significant when I was a sophomore and enjoying more floor time than the previous year. We were preparing to play Buhl in semi-final play in our District 28 Tournament action. Buhl had defeated us twice during the year and a lot of their wins were engineered by Dick Panyan, their lightning-quick guard. Coach

Richard W. Varichak

Roels felt that the way to stop Panyan was to keep him from getting the ball. He instructed Bob Altavilla and me to alternate defending Panyan and not to let him near the basketball. For two to three minutes apiece, Bob and I would "dog" him all over the floor and Coach Roels, in his last command, said, "If he goes to the bathroom, go with him! Don't leave his side!" Well, the strategy worked to perfection. Panyan could only collect two points, both on free throws and it would have been nice to say we pulled out the win. But alas! Our offense went south and we lost 24-22. I used this strategy years later when I was coaching the Hibbing Junior College basketball team. We had to go to Ely to play a tough Ely Junior College squad, led by sharp-shooting Tony Bartovich. I put two of my quickest players on Tony, they restricted him to a measly four points, and we did go on to win. The coach of the Ely team was Bob Altavilla, the teammate who helped me tie up Dick Panyan 18 years earlier. What irony! I loved it!

    Although Swede Pergol did a wonderful job in developing me and my baseball teammates into an American Legion power, it took a young ex-marine and our swimming coach to lead us to a State High School Championship. Bill Loushine was an ex-Bluestreak all-around athlete who went on to get his college and teaching degree at Lacrosse College in Wisconsin. When we qualified for the State High School baseball playoffs in 1948 he was appointed as our coach. Bill was a strict disciplinarian and wanted us to "toe the line." After coming off Swede Pergol's laid back leadership, some team members didn't like the change. But Coach Loushine recognized the athleticism and potential of our team and proceeded to teach us advanced skills which he had performed at the college level. One of our favorite moves came with opponents on second and third and two outs. To start the play, catcher Rudy Kne would step out of the catcher's box and pretend to fix his leg straps This alerted me at third and Dick Quaal at second base. On the next pitch, Kne would rifle the ball down to me at third. The runner at third usually hustled back to the base in time, but he was not the base runner we were after. Upon receiving Rudy's throw, I immediately whipped the ball to Quaal at second who, most of the time, caught the runner sleeping and not

Fifty-Five Years on the Bench

expecting the ball to come his way. This move got us out of several innings in which we could have given up a bunch of runs.

Another teaching tool offered by Coach Loushine was the situation involving opponent runners on first and third. If the runner on first broke for second, Rudy would throw down to second. If the runner on third decided to come home, Quaal at second base would intercept the throw behind the pitcher's mound and throw the runner out at home plate. If the runner stayed at third, Quaal would let the ball go to Altavilla covering second to tag the runner coming from first.

Figure 6: Chisholm Free Press photo
Coach Bill Loushine

But one of Loushine's greatest decisions came in our opening quarter final game in the baseball state tournament against Austin High School. They had just won the American Legion State Championship a few weeks earlier and probably thought they wouldn't have too much trouble in handling those "farmers from the north." We started George Hudak, our fire-balling right hander, but Austin was a good fastball hitting club. They hit George pretty hard and built up a 4-1 lead after four innings. Coach Loushine then brought in Dick Anderson, with the complete opposite of Hudak's offerings. I don't think Dick's fastball could break a pane of glass, but his ball did some weird things on the way to home plate. It was almost laughable to watch the heavy hitters from Austin breaking their backs trying to hit Anderson's deliveries. Hudak later hit a grand slam homerun and we went on to win 10-7. The Austin team was so devastated by the loss they packed up their bags and went home, thus forfeiting their games in the consolation bracket. For this ill-advised action, the Austin program was put on a one year suspension.

Richard W. Varichak

Anderson went on to pitch a five hitter the next night as we edged St. Paul Washington 3-1. Hudak completed the three game sweep by handcuffing Springfield High School in the championship game 13-8. Bill Loushine gave me another building block in his philosophy of discipline and detail coverage.

As I left the halls of Chisholm High School to go on to the University of Minnesota-Duluth, I was introduced to a couple more basketball coaches who reflected the positive aspects of the coaching and teaching profession. Recruited to play at the U of MN-Duluth, I first came in contact with Jim Hastings, our freshman coach. Jim, who later on would be a highly successful coach at Duluth Central, was a grad student working on his Masters Degree as a member of the Bulldog Staff. He was a quiet type of mentor who became close to his players. He never raised his voice and kept an even temperament no matter if we won or lost- truly a players' coach.

The varsity coach, Ray Isenbarger, proved to be much tougher on his players, but was a good drill master and a smart bench coach. I found out personally that Coach Isenbarger wanted you to follow his directions to the letter. After playing the forward slot on my Chisholm team, I had to learn the skills of a guard and to sharpen up my outside shooting. He warned me about driving to the basket too much, as I had done in high school. My lesson to be learned occurred the night we played host to the St. Cloud Huskies. Disregarding his warning about driving to the basket against bigger opponents, that is exactly what I did. On the drive down the lane, I met up with a 6'9" center's elbow which floored me, broke my nose, and decorated my game jersey with a bloody background. As I lay on the floor, quite stunned, surrounded by my teammates and the team trainer, I heard coach remark, "You dumb Bohunk, I told you not to drive so much." He then walked off the court and directed the trainer to take me to the training room for repairs. He taught me the acceptance of injuries and how to react to individual cases- don't get too excited or over-whelmed when one of your players suffers an injury or illness.

Fifty-Five Years on the Bench

I also found out the importance of academic eligibility and how it affects not only the player, but also the coaching staff. Midway through my freshman season, I fell to the rigors of class work and was declared ineligible for the rest of the season. I felt bad for a failure to dedicate myself to my college education, but also for disappointing the two coaches who had put a lot of time and effort to make me a better athlete.

After leaving UMD and serving a tour of underground mining, my next educational stop was at Hibbing Junior College. A coaching legend was in the wings, waiting to give me some more valuable insight in the profession. Joe Milinovich coached the football and basketball teams and the Cardinals had been highly successful in both sports. Much to the dismay of my father, I donned football pads and planned on carrying the Cardinal colors on the gridiron. Little did I realize I would be carrying not only colors but the football as well, because coach Milinovich said I would be the starting fullback. After playing the end position in high school, I had to learn quickly how to run the ball, find the hole, run through it, and block defending linemen who wanted to crucify Myrle Rice, our gifted quarterback. My transformation from end to fullback proved to be a coaching success as I led the team in rushing, was second in scoring, and earned a place on the All-Conference Team. Coach Milinovich taught me more about the game of football in one fall of competition than I experienced in four years of my high school games.

Joe also handled the basketball program and although a superior motivator, was not as strong as he was a football leader. He gave us a few options, a basic defense, and then sat back to enjoy our efforts in ringing up a 26-2 record and a third place finish in the Region 13 playoffs. I was the point guard on our 1-4 offensive lineup which also included Frank Bay at 6'1", Leo Hartman at 6'5", Dan Lastovich at 6'4", and Dick Garmaker at 6'4". Garmaker would go on to gain All-American honors at the University of Minnesota and then perform with the Minneapolis Lakers and New York Knicks on the NBA level. Joe always "had a dream" and sometimes these dreams led to unbelievable happenings on the football field and the basketball court. My lessons from Joe involved motivation, "dreams" and athletic creativity. The final word on Joe

Richard W. Varichak

Milinovich - he helped me get my super job at Hibbing Junior College 12 years later.

Figure 7: Photo by Arnie Maki - Hibbing Junior College, 1964
Coach Joe Milinovich with Coach Dick Varichak

One thing I learned as a coach and teacher, you are never too old or experienced to still learn. I have experienced additional learning not only from my former coaches but also from players of mine who have entered the coaching world. Doug Schmitz and I have been coaching together for twenty years and I have benefitted from his vast knowledge of basketball and baseball. Serving as his assistant coach in high school girls' basketball has been a fulfilling addition to my coaching life. He could easily coach on the Division I or II level. My baseball knowledge was enhanced by two of my former baseball stars at Hibbing J.C. John Anderson pitched for me for one year before he went south to play and coach with the University of Minnesota Gophers. I learned a little about

Fifty-Five Years on the Bench

pitching from both Anderson and Schmitz. I recognized that Tim Scott, who was my catcher at Hibbing J.C., would be a coach once he finished college. He served as Hibbing High School's baseball coach for many years. He also doubled as Hibbing's Athletic Director and was my boss when I became involved with the girls' basketball program.

Each of the aforementioned gentlemen contributed important building blocks in my quest for a teaching and coaching life. I've used their strengths and dropped their weaknesses (which were few) to build my own coaching philosophy. I will always be in their debt for over a half a century of coaching enjoyment and involvement with the finest young student athletes in the world.

Chapter 4: Male and Female Athletes Play on Different Planes

Prior to getting my first public school coaching assignment at Evant, Texas, I completed seven years as a coach with military teams and with men's' sports programs at the University of Texas. The Evant job gave me my first opportunity to coach girls' sports and introduced me to a different athletic environment.

I was hired at Evant High School to lead the girls' basketball team, which in 1960, featured six girl squads on the floor. Three guards and three forwards played only on their end of the floor and could not cross the centerline at midcourt. Basically, the game was played three on three and much different in strategy than the traditional five on five which the boys still played. On our game nights the girls and their three on three teams played in the first contest, followed by the boys with their five on five set up. I didn't have any trouble with the boys' game, but had to learn how to direct a three on three offense and defense with my girls. My first big decision as the girls coach was to move a senior guard named Carolyn Arnold to forward. She had great quickness, could score from anywhere on the court and possessed unusual heady court sense. When informed of my decision to change her position, Carolyn pleaded with me, "Oh Coach, don't move me to forward, I can't score." She was afraid to disappoint me and felt her comfort level was at the guard position. Once Carolyn adjusted to her new position she became a scoring machine and turned into one of the top girl cagers in the state. She definitely was one of the top five players that I ever had the pleasure to coach.

My other decision was to move a 5'10" sophomore, Marcia (Marsay) Buster into my starting lineup at a guard slot. Marcia was tremendously strong, a farm girl, very quick and aggressive. But she had to learn the game. She proved to be a demon on defense and made my decision look good. Her reaction to my decision was to deliver the biggest hug I

Fifty-Five Years on the Bench

ever received. This was to be the first of many hugs I have received over the past 50 years from emotional girl athletes.

My role as a girls coach evolved in different phases as the years rolled by. With my girls at Evant and later at Darrouzett High School in Darrouzett Texas, I became a big brother figure. I wasn't too much older than my players and we more or less shared the culture of that time period. However, in my position as coach of the 1991-1992 Hibbing Cardinals Junior College team, I became a father figure. I was 60 years old now and gray was slowly dotting my hair line. Players were not afraid to ask me questions and sometimes doubted my decisions. I enjoyed this special group of college players as they worked hard and were fun to be around. We had only six players, so at times, because of the five-foul ejection rule we ended up with only 3 players at the conclusion of the game.

In my thirteen years coaching girls' basketball, I discovered some acute differences between male and female athletes. I want to emphasize that the following comments are only my observations and come from my own experience with both boys and girls basketball players. My own participation in basketball stretched from elementary school competition to junior high, varsity, college, and military play. I competed with individuals who I was not close to and some I just didn't like. Off the court I did not socialize or speak very often to those teammates I didn't care for. This antagonism disappeared completely when we suited up for practice and games. All negative feelings for each other were put aside and team work was the main focus in our play. I found this behavior was true with the boys' teams I coached, with one exception I will discuss described in a later chapter. So there was no worry about jealousy and hard feelings during the games.

Not so with my girl athletes! From my first job at Evant to my final years with our Hibbing High School Blue Jackets, I did observe some instances where female teammates who harbored negative feelings toward another carried those feelings onto the court. As a coaching staff, it was imperative that we recognized this situation and quickly took action to rectify it. In Darrouzett, I had to sit two of my starters for the simple reason they forgot that the other one was on the floor. We basically were playing with four players. After a couple of games with this situation, I had to take some action. I benched both girls and explained to them that unless their court behavior changed, they would watch the games from the bench. Both girls were seniors, very competitive, and wanted no part of sitting. They started playing together and our team chemistry improved dramatically.

When we were eliminated from district play in Darrouzett, I faced another disciplinary problem brought around by one of my junior guards. Upset with the loss, she later poured a bottle of Coca-Cola over one of the girls who was on the club that beat us. This was done while both were in the stands watching the next game after the completion of our contest. This episode brought a heated request by the coach and administration of the school involved for us to take some action, and discipline our player. After a special school board meeting I was instructed to make a decision on what disciplinary action to be taken. As the high school principal, responsible for student discipline, I suspended the girl for three days which eventually kept her from claiming the valedictorian honor for the school. She did end up as salutatorian, but several years later at an All-Class reunion, she did come up to me, gave me a big hug and told me that I was entirely correct in my decision concerning her suspension.

I faced this dilemma only once with the Hibbing girls. It was in my first year as an assistant varsity coach. Unfortunately, no action was taken and our team chemistry was not the best throughout the season. Not many wins, quite a few blowout losses, but I still enjoyed coaching a granddaughter.

Coaching pleasure in Hibbing commenced with a later team, our 7th grade girls who Coach Doug Schmitz and I have labeled our "fab nine." They stayed with each other for six years, had great chemistry and took us to State Tournament competition in their senior year. More about the "Fab Nine" in chapter nine.

A small difference between the two genders also surfaced at practice sessions. For the most part my girls' teams were avid learners. I

Fifty-Five Years on the Bench

usually used the term "like sponges." The girls seem to enjoy the basketball education they were receiving and reflected this learning in their work ethic. I did get this attention from most of my boys' teams but there seemed to be a hesitation in their acceptance of basketball learning. More questions were asked by the males and the attitude, "Oh yes, I know that," was often present.

With my first boys' team in Evant, we were going through a period of our season schedule where we were having a tough time scoring. Shots were not falling and our kids were getting pretty frustrated. With my patience getting thin listening to their excuses for the ball failing to slip through the hoop, I brought out the fact that two basketballs, side by side, can fit through the basket. I then followed this statement with the remark, "If two balls can fit through the hoop, you guys certainly can fit one through." They laughed at this suggestion until I brought out a ladder and two basketballs. I then proceeded to slip both balls through the hoop and it was my turn to laugh as I saw the amazed looks on their faces. Girls, on the other hand, readily accepted my explanation when I had used the "two-ball" through the hoop remark.

So, the bottom line in my experience with both boys and girls is that I thoroughly enjoyed both of them and the difference in attitudes, behavior, and emotion made coaching an unforgettable pleasure.

I found the guiding principles on coaching males and females extremely interesting when introduced by Competitive Advantage of Amherst, Massachusetts. I feel the opinions expressed in this study are important and I am glad to include them in this chapter.

Richard W. Varichak

Coaching Males & Females Guiding Principles[1]

SOCIALIZATION OF MALES: Little boys are socialized to be aggressive, loud, competitive, dominant, independent, and to be comfortable standing out. As a coach, you need to also train them to be more cooperative, team-oriented, unselfish, empathetic and socially related.

SOCIALIZATION OF FEMALES: Little girls are socialized to be dependent, quiet, passive, cooperative, team and other oriented, emotive and non-selfish. As a coach you need to train them to be aggressive, competitive, "selfish," dominant and independent.

FEMALES "SPEAK" THE RELATIONSHIP LANGUAGE: Females are relationship oriented. To be successful and effective with young women, you must understand that the coach-athlete relationship is THE most important organizing factor for them. Your relationship with your female athletes is the primary vehicle that conveys all of your teaching. When there is a conflict or problem with your relationship, this must be immediately addressed and resolved before any useful teaching can continue.

MALES ARE TASK ORIENTED: Young men tend to be much more focused on the job at hand. They are less likely to get distracted by coach-athlete conflicts. While the relationship with you is important to them, they are still able to pay attention to what you want them to do, even when they are upset with you or you are upset with them.

DO NOT USE "IN YOUR FACE" TACTICS WITH FEMALES: While you may be able to effectively motivate young men by being loud, angry and "in your face", these tactics will immediately shut down most of your female athletes. Screaming at young women distracts them from the content of your message and gets them to focus on what is wrong with their relationship with you. Regardless of how angry or frustrated you may be, you must maintain control of your emotions and continue to speak the "relationship language."

YOUR RELATIONSHIP DETERMINES YOUR COACHING EFFECTIVENESS: The quality of the individual relationships that you develop with your athletes, male and female, will ultimately determine how successful and effective you are as a coach. How you treat them, what you say to them, and how you say it, will determine whether they feel that you are trustworthy and worth listening to. Are you honest? Do you speak clearly what's on your mind? Are you a good listener? Are you supportive? Can you set clear and appropriate limits? Are you open to appropriate feedback?

BE FLEXIBLE FOR MAXIMUM COACHING EFFECTIVENESS: Whether you're coaching males or females, your effectiveness as a coach lies in your ability to be flexible in how you approach your athletes. Be willing to treat every athlete on your squad uniquely, as an individual. Be willing to adjust your approach and coaching technique to fit the individual that you are working with at that moment. Because every athlete on your team is different, what turns one athlete on, shuts another off. Take the time early on to figure out what makes each athlete tick and it will pay big dividends for you later.

YOU CAN'T NOT DEVELOP A COACH-ATHLETE RELATIONSHIP: Good or bad, you are always developing a relationship with your athletes. Whether you do this by yelling and screaming, gentle support or by totally ignoring an athlete doesn't matter. You are always "building" relationships. The quality of these relationships is largely dependent upon how aware or conscious you are of what you are doing as you interact with your athletes on a daily basis. If you are not aware of how your behavior affects an individual or the team, then your relationship building will not be in your control, and therefore you will be much less successful as a coach. Remember, everything that you say and do with your athletes affects them positively or negatively and determines the quality of your relationship.

FEMALES STRUGGLE WITH THE "BEST VS. LIKEABLE" CONFLICT: The female athlete had a constant battle waging within her between wanting to be the best and stand-out, and her concern for what this will mean to her social standing in the group. Because of her need for social acceptance, the female athlete does not want to rock the boat with her strivings for excellence. Your job as a coach is to help the female athlete feel comfortable going for it without getting distracted by what her friends might think.

CREATE A SAFE ENVIRONMENT ON YOUR TEAM FOR WOMEN TO EXCEL: Encourage the women on your team to compete hard and actively pursue excellence. Make it clear to all that this is not only acceptable, but desired behavior on your squad. Do not collude with or allow athlete behaviors that scape-goat the individual that may be excelling. Go out of your way to set clear and firm limits preventing social behavior that discourages the individual pursuit of excellence.

TEACH COMPETITION AS A "WIN-WIN" PROPOSITION: This is especially important when working with female athletes. You need to help your athletes understand that one teammate's success is NOT another's failure. On the contrary! When a teammate out competes her mates, it provides them with both a model of excellence and the motivational incentive to pursue that model. This positive "reframe" of within-team competition is absolutely critical for your ultimate success when working with women. The new message that must get communicated is that "if you really care about your teammate, you will do everything in your power to kick her butt!"

DRIVE MALES, LEAD FEMALES: In general, males are led more effectively by a powerful, aggressive presence driving them. Status and intimidation are often quite effective motivators for the male athlete, who

Fifty-Five Years on the Bench

you have to convince of your expertise and authority. With males you must somehow earn their respect. Females are better led by a coach with the ability to communicate a sense of caring for the athlete that transcends that athlete's individual abilities on the field. The female athlete does not need to be convinced of your knowledge and expertise. She will give you the benefit of the doubt. What you must convince her of however is that you genuinely care about her as a person.

PROVIDING CRITICAL FEEDBACK: FEMALES: When you approach a female team with criticism, everyone on that squad thinks that you are personally talking to them. In general, the female athlete takes on far too much responsibility for things when they go wrong. Add to this a tendency to exaggerate her weaknesses and minimize her strengths and you have an athlete with inaccurately low self-esteem. When you provide important, negative feedback, you need to keep this in mind. Be specific and clear with you feedback, making sure that the athlete has heard exactly what you intended for her to hear. At the same time, try to also underline what that athlete did positively.

PROVIDING CRITICAL FEEDBACK: MALES: Your typical male athlete is much more highly defended than his female counterpart. What this means is that male athletes are less likely to believe that negative feedback directed at them, really belongs to them. They instead believe that their teammates are more responsible for the mistake or problem. In this way the male athlete tends to externalize blame and responsibility. This comes out of an unrealistically optimistic assessment of his skill and ability level. Sometimes the most effective way to provide negative feedback to male athletes is to present them with hard facts: video replay of the behavior/performance you want to correct.

Chapter 5: Evant Elks

Wow! My college studies are over- for awhile! August 1960 I now own a Master of Education degree from the University of Texas and I am ready to go to work. During the second semester of my graduate work in 1960 I made many trips down to the Teacher Employment Office in Sutton Hall to check on open educational positions. Teaching jobs were numerous that year and I knew I would have quite a few choices. School administrators were always in the office trying to recruit personnel who were looking for employment.

A high school principal from Houston captured me on one of my trips to the Employment Office and stated he was seeking a basketball coach and a physics instructor. When I informed him I was not physics major he said the school district would send me to school to get the proper credentials. He wasn't the only administrator who wanted to shanghai me, but none of the positions interested me. Finally I found the situation which did interest me and I settled on contacting Evant School District, a small Class B school about 60 miles west of Waco and 100 miles north of Austin.

In May I took my wife Noka and daughter, Vikki (3 ½ years old) up to Evant for my interview. I thought the interview was very positive and my chance of being hired was good. I think the clincher to my being hired was orchestrated by my beautiful daughter as she climbed into the lap of the board president and innocently inquired, "Are you going to give my daddy a job?" That "brought the house down," so to speak, as the board members all joined together in hearty laughter. It wasn't too much longer that the board notified me that I was selected to teach and coach at the home of the Elks!

Noka and Vikki remained in Austin because of her job while my son Tom and I made the trek to Evant to begin house hunting and prepare for the start of football practice. My wife and daughter joined us

Fifty-Five Years on the Bench

at the end of August and we were a family again. I think Tom was glad to see Mom as he wasn't too enthralled with my culinary efforts.

The football program had been in the depths of a few losing seasons and I found out early that the boys had not received the best of coaching efforts. I couldn't believe they lacked certain skills, such as how to lineup for kickoffs, footwork with our backs, and offensive techniques. Coming from the U of Texas Longhorns, I felt we would copy Darrel Royals wishbone offense. I found some good athletes who I believed could operate this offense and I started teaching it.

Figure 8: Photo by Eddie Hudgins - Evant Gazzette
1960 Evant High School Football Coaches
Assistant Coach Pantelano Moreno, Assistant Coach Don Barkley, and Head Coach Dick Varichak

Ervin Koerth and David Lovelace were the two best athletes on the team, with Lovelace handling the quarterback position and Koerth our featured running back. Clynton Smith, at 6'2" and 250 pounds, anchored our lines while Eldon Perkins, my 145 pound center, proved to be a rugged tiger, both on offense and defense.

Richard W. Varichak

After our first game, a 30-0 loss, I found out we did not have the personnel to run the wishbone. We switched to a winged "T" and I discovered another coaching secret: you pattern your attack and team philosophy to the caliber of your team members! It would be nice to say we went undefeated the rest of the season, but that would not be. We did win two, tied one and lost seven, the best record the Elks had achieved in the past three years. Our offense was better than our defense and once again I found out that defensive coaching, in the past, was lacking. Not being a defensive specialist myself, this lack of defensive knowledge didn't improve too much.

Sometimes it takes only one play to certify a coach as a so-called "genius." This happened to me in our game against Goldthwaite, a neighboring Class "A" school. On a rainy, miserable night at Goldthwaite, our two teams were battling to a scoreless tie. We almost pulled out the win on a miscommunication play between our quarterback Dave Lovelace and me. With just three minutes left in the game, we had a punting situation from our 45 yard line. I motioned with my leg to punt the ball, but Lovelace thought I signaled for a fake punt. Koerth, our punter, took the snap, faked the punt, handing off to Lovelace who came around from a split end position. I nearly had a heart attack when I saw what was developing, but Lovelace completed the fake and raced down to the Goldthwaite two yard line before he was knocked out of bounds. Although the fake punt worked to perfection and we had a chance to score, we suffered a fumble on the next play and lost the ball. The final score remained at a 0-0 tie when time ran out. But the play was the talk of the town and parents and townspeople marveled at my strategy to attempt such a trick play in spite of weather conditions. I never did admit to not calling the play. I just sat back and let my team and fans think I was a heck of a coach!

After the final game against Hico in which we took a 48-8 pasting, I was a little downhearted on the bus ride home. I lightened up somewhat when Ervin Koerth, one of our best football players, came up to me and said, "Coach, I want to tell you I learned more football this year, than all the other years put together. I can't thank you enough."

Fifty-Five Years on the Bench

Koerth topped off his great play by being named the most valuable player in the conference. What a proud moment for both of us and the Evant football program.

Now I had to draw double duty when the basketball season came around. As head coach for both the girls and boys teams, I had to learn the nuances of 3 on 3 offense and defense with my girls. The boys still employed the normal 5 on 5 games with which I was most familiar. On game nights, the girls played the opener and the boys contest immediately followed. I thought that the boys program would be strong with football aces, Lovelace and Koerth, along with 6'5" center, Jimmy Blackburn, all three returning starters. It was the girls programs of which I was not sure. Only two seniors returned, Carolyn Arnold and Kathy Parrish, a guard and a sharp-shooting forward. During our first few days of drills, I discovered Carolyn had some tremendous offensive skills. She was lightning fast and could score from anywhere on the court. I had Kathy and Rosalyn Koerth as two of my starting forwards, but lacked a good third. Then the light bulb went off and I had my third good forward- Carolyn! When I told her of my decision, she reared back in surprise and exclaimed, "Oh Coach, don't move me to forward. I can't score." Carolyn had been a guard for the past three years and that was her comfort level. She was outstanding at the guard position but I wondered how her last coach missed her shooting and scoring potential. Although we lost her athleticism and quickness at guard, the cupboard wasn't bare. Connie Armstrong returned as a starter and proved to be a heady, tough defender. Raye Atchley became a blue collar player, very physical and highly competitive. I moved a young sophomore, Marcia Buster into the starting lineup, a 5'11" dynamo who made the game interesting for me because of her sometimes wild play. I could use her, always on the best offensive opponent.

Once Carolyn adjusted to her new position, she became our scoring machine. While Carolyn gave us all-around offense, Kathy provided our strong outside shooting game. Rosalyn was our power forward, was a tenacious rebounder, and cleaned up any missed shots by our other two forwards.

Richard W. Varichak

Carolyn not only was a top-notch athlete, she also excelled in the classroom. A 4.0 student since first grade, she became Evant's 1961 valedictorian. She followed in her mother's footsteps as her mother, Lenore, also was a 4.0 student and ended up as valedictorian. Carolyn, in her graduation address, gave the same speech her mother gave many years before. Besides serving as co-captain of the basketball team, she was elected head cheerleader and was involved in student government and school yearbook. She was the finest example of a student athlete in my professional career and remains a close friend today, 49 years later. I consider her one of my top five basketball players I have had the pleasure of coaching.

She also played a part in one of my most embarrassing moments as a coach. In one of our home games I had her on the bench to give her a well-deserved rest. She didn't come off the floor many times! When she told me she was ready to go back in I gave her the okay and as she passed me I unconsciously gave her a pat on her gluteus maximus. She stopped short, turned to me and asked, "Coach! Did you pat me on the butt?" She had a shocked look on her face and I went looking for the nearest hole to dive into. The crowd chuckled and the team members broke out in controlled laughter. Another coaching tip! – You don't pat a girl basketball player on her behind! Carolyn and I still have a laugh over that incident.

Three more serious incidents happened on our basketball court and involved my girls. During one of our home game contests against Lometa H.S., a bitter rival we love to defeat, one of our older fans started to choke and fell to the floor from his bleacher seat. He was seated behind our bench so I rushed to his side to administer CPR and I was joined by the wife of the Lometa coach, who was a nurse. We spent some time trying to revive him, but it became obvious that he was gone. After the EMT personnel and ambulance left the game was resumed, but it lost all its luster and excitement. We won the game eventually, but it seemed like a hollow win. The fan was an avid sports follower who owned our local hardware store.

Fifty-Five Years on the Bench

Figure 9: Photo by A.E. Greer
1960-61 Evant Elks
Front row (l to r): Pam Peays, Connie Armstrong, Raye Atchley, Marsa Waddell, Linda Kay Elam. Middle row: Irma Sue Williams, Carolyn Arnold, Kathy Parrish, Ann Wagner, Betty Jane Faubion. Back row: Kay Belvin (mgr.), Charlotte Sheldon, Marcia Buster, Patricia Townsend, Patsy Conner, Rosalyn Koerth, Coach Dick Varichak.

Another low point for our girls was the accidental drowning of Connie Armstrong's dad while fishing. Connie was a strong, young lady who was emotionally upset with her dad's death, but continued to be very dedicated and valuable to our program. Connie and I still keep in touch with each other and I relish her company after all these years.

Another one of the guards, Patsy Conner, found out her father was terminally ill. This was the night of a home game and I could see she was terribly affected by the news but insisted she could play. It was evident that the situation was too much for her, so I had her go home after the first half. The rest of the game was played in a somber manner although we did manage to eke out a victory.

Another lesson learned at the coaching level: you share the wins and highs that come to you and your team, but you also share the sadness

Richard W. Varichak

and sorrow that sometimes works into your schedules of teaching and coaching. This is part of the coaching profession, and I found that I was fully involved in this responsibility.

The girls did Evant H.S. and themselves proud in the year 1960-61 as they carved out an 18-10 record. This included winning two invitational tournaments, winning the District Championship, and ending up fourth in Regional play, two games away from State Tourney competition.

Our boys' team basically matched the output of our girls' team in establishing an 18-9 record and a District Crown. We didn't have the scoring power of a Carolyn Arnold, but with all five starters able to score, we passed the point totals around. Jimmy Blackburn, our 6'5" pivot led most of our scoring, but Dave Lovelace, from his point guard slot and Ervin Koerth, our power forward, contributed their share of scores. Lovelace was the most versatile player on the team. At 6'2" and owning considerable court sense, he ran our offense, but he also was the best defender we had.

One of my learning tools proved to be the camera to record games. Our school couldn't afford a camera, so normally we didn't use game films. In our home games with Hamilton H.S., a double A school sixteen miles away, we did have our contests filmed through the courtesy of our opponent. In our first contest in Hamilton, we received a physical whipping to the tune of 81-61. Spearheading this rout were by two giants on the front line, a 6'9" center, Don McCaleb with 35 points, and their 6'9" forward, Ernie Sandell with 17 scores, along with Don Thompson, their talented point guard, who threw in 19 points. I requested the game film from Coach Jones and studied it for a week prior to our next meeting in Evant. Very noticeable was that Thompson was the key to running their offense and getting the ball to the big boys. When we prepared for them, I took Dave Lovelace aside and gave him instructions to get in Thompson's face, remembering what Coach Harvey Roels told me to do against Dick Panyon and Buhl some 24 years earlier, "If he goes to the bathroom, you go with him- don't leave him!"

Fifty-Five Years on the Bench

Lovelace played the defensive game of his career- not letting Thompson near the ball and limiting him to three points. But Thompson could not get the ball to McCaleb and Sandell as they tallied only 19

Figure 10: Photo by A.E. Greer
1960-61 Evant Elks
Front row (l to r): John Griggs, Glen Price, Larry Hodo, Gene Lane, Jimmy Gholson, Mike Flach. Middle row: Ross Conner, E.J. Belvin, Bryan Parrish, Tommy Smith, James Billingsley, William Thompson. Back row: Gary Marwitz (mgr.), Jimmy Blackburn, Clynton Smith, Coach Dick Varichak, Ervin Koerth, David Lovelace, Eldon Perkins (mgr.).

points between them. Alas! We still lost but the margin was 63-61 and once again my team thought I was a coaching magician.

I found the tough part of coaching dealing with a couple of parents that first year. In our Bi-District playoff game it went down to the wire before we won by a couple of points. Late in the first half, my center got in foul trouble and I had to sit him. I put in Bill Thompson, a 6'3" sophomore, who did a nice job with Blackburn on the bench. After the win I was on cloud nine when I found out that was the furthest any Elk Team had advanced. The next morning while I was in my 8:00 a.m. Economics class, Superintendent Alfred Greer came in and wanted to see me in his office. When I walked into his office, an irate father shouted, "I should punch you in the nose!" He was the dad of one of my reserves who didn't get in the game and was angry because I used a sophomore instead of his boy, who was a junior. His son was a mediocre athlete, a starter for me in football, but was not a very good basketball player. I couldn't convince the father that his son was only reserve material and the game situation did not call for his participation. This incident caused a personal rift between me and the family, and we were never close after that.

Another dad who became upset with me was not aware of Texas State High School rules. His son was a little used reserve on my football team, and I had a difficult time finding a position for him. He just was not a football player, but played because his friends were on the team. Midway through the season he was caught drinking at a party and I had to remove him from the squad. The father, a school board member, became upset, although I was following Texas State H.S. rules. This animosity towards me extended to the hiring of teachers for the next year. I was eventually rehired on a 6-1 vote, and you guessed it, he voted to fire me, even though my evaluation from the administration was highly positive with their recommendation to rehire me. This action brought about my resignation after the next year as I had always told my wife that if I didn't get a unanimous vote from the Board I would move on. Thus, I did spend one more year at Evant and then resigned.

I immediately found a position with Darrouzett High School in north Texas, serving as a Teaching Principal and girls' basketball coach. This was also a class B school, even smaller than Evant, but it gave me a chance to try out my H.S. principal's role and kept me in girls' basketball coaching We weren't very good on the basketball court, but the kids worked hard and they were fun to work around. I made a lot of friends with dedicated parents who did not care for the superintendent. They fired him at the conclusion of the school year and asked me to take the post. I refused the option because I felt I was too inexperienced for the job but was rehired as girls' basketball coach and principal.

Fifty-Five Years on the Bench

In March I received a call from Hibbing Junior College and was offered a college teaching and coaching position, thanks to my old coach, Joe Milinovich. Noka and I did not hesitate to accept the job and then spent 29 great years in a college experience, which also brought me back to Minnesota's Iron Range.

It's been 49 years since I entered the halls of Evant High School and the two memorable years which gave me ultimate confidence in my teaching and coaching career. Sometimes the first year of teaching and coaching will dictate whether one stays in the field. If the experience proves to be negative, the first year instructor will seek another vocation. Fortunately my tenure at Evant motivated me to further pursue a teaching and coaching profession.

I have to include here my two administrators who gave me guidance, loyalty, and believed in my athletic philosophy. Alfred Greer was only 31 years old as our superintendent at Evant and proved to be a no-nonsense leader who also possessed a fine sense of humor. Shortly after we came to Evant, Alfred invited us over for a round-steak meal. I was already salivating with the thought of digesting a nice thick steak. Much to our surprise when we arrived at the Greer residence with appetites at a high level, we got our round steak- bologna sandwiches! We still laugh at Alfred's humor. I miss him. He was a pleasure to work with, as was Harold Acker, our pint-sized principal. Harold, although vertically challenged, had a quick mind and was extremely personable. He later replaced Greer as superintendant which was a good move for Harold and the school district.

Fortunately I've been able to keep in contact with a few players and enjoyed two reunions with them. We shared memories with each other and I found out many things of which I was unaware. Thank heavens, they were all positive. Maybe they did not want to bring up any negatives. At one of the reunions, as we toured the new school addition, Carolyn Arnold and I decided to sneak into the old gym to shoot some baskets. This was in the summer so the main doors were locked. We found an open window where we squeezed in and went looking for balls. Lo and behold, we saw a rack of balls on the court sideline and proceed-

Richard W. Varichak

ed to cast all kinds of shot attempts. I observed very quickly that Carolyn had not lost her shooting touch and thought to myself, "This young lady could put on a uniform and score at will!" We both laughed at our action that afternoon and thought what a newspaper headline could read- "Former Coach and Player Arrested for Breaking in Evant Gym." Another great memory with my favorite player!

As a retired teacher and coach, I always will be indebted to Evant, Texas. These outstanding players and parents gave me the jump start to enjoy a lifetime desire to be a part of a great educational process. Go Elks!!!

Figure 12: Photo by A.E. Greer
Carolyn Arnold – Senior, Captain, Forward, All-District

Figure 11: Photo by A.E. Greer
Kathy Parrish - Senior, Forward

Figure 14: Photo by A.E. Greer
Raye Atchley - Junior, Guard

Figure 13: Photo by A.E. Greer
Connie Armstrong - Junior, Guard

Fifty-Five Years on the Bench

Figure 16: Photo by A.E. Greer
Rosalyn Koerth - Sophomore, Forward

Figure 16: Photo by A.E. Greer
Marcia Buster - Sophomore, Guard

Figure 15: Photo by A.E. Greer
Vikki Varichak - Ball Girl

Figure 19: Photo by Evant I.S. D. 1961
A. E. Greer - The Boss
Superintendent of Evant School District

Chapter 6: Doug Schmitz – A Study in Perfection Required

One of the best experiences which surfaces in the coaching profession is the discovery of new friends. Due to my job at Hibbing Community College I had the opportunity to gather many new colleagues and friends. And, as it happens so often, life-long relationships tend to bloom. That's how Doug Schmitz came into our life.

Doug was a 1972 graduate of Sebeka High School, where he was an all-around athlete and honor student. He was a surprise enrollee who now resided in Pengilly, about 15 miles from Hibbing. His parents had moved to Pengilly in his junior year, but he opted to live with his grandparents until he graduated from Sebeka. I really didn't know he was around until my dad informed me that one of his work study students could really shoot a basketball. My dad, George, was a custodian at the college and his work station was the gymnasium. Doug was assigned to him as a work study student and sweet-talked my dad into giving him a basketball so he could shoot baskets during his lunch break. So, one evening when we had my parents over for dinner, my dad told me about Doug and what he could do with a basketball. I had to look for myself. When I observed him during his solo shooting period, I thought we sure could use him on the college team.

Our first meeting occurred in the faculty mail room when he approached me and told me he was going to try out for the college team. I encouraged him to come out for the squad and this began a 37-year relationship. Along with Doug, I was fortunate to attain the services of ex-Bluejacket cagers, Rick Stark, Bob Eggers, and Bob Walker. Lou Janezich and Tom Gornick came over from Chisholm, so I figured we could have a pretty good year. Returning letter winners Tom Ronchetti, Scott Johnson, Kevin Orak, and Gary Peterson gave the Cardinals a good sophomore base.

We didn't win any championships in Doug's two years, but I saw him grow by leaps and bounds as a college athlete and student. Being an honor student in high school, he wanted to be an engineer, so he enrolled

Fifty-Five Years on the Bench

in our pre-engineering program. He didn't get the best counseling from the department and was given classes that put him in over his head as a first quarter freshman. He pleaded with me to help him out and, seeing his potential as a teacher and coach, I persuaded him to go into the educational field as a Physical Educator. His wife Kathy also suggested a P.ED. Major, so he didn't hesitate to make the change. As his advisor and physical education instructor, I had him in quite a few classes. I found him to be a bright and enthusiastic student who often did more in class than he was assigned to do. He showed leadership qualities right away in our basketball and baseball programs. I had him assigned as my work study student, which didn't make my dad very happy. It seems he was one of Dad's best workers and he would miss him. Doug also became my right hand man with our Intramural program. In fact, I could toss him my keys, go home for dinner, and never worry about how the activities were operating. I made up my mind that once he got his B.S. degree and I had the chance, I would recommend his hiring with us at Hibbing Community College.

Doug was an extreme pleasure to coach because of his work ethic, enthusiasm, intelligence, and of course, his talent. He was not a starter in his freshman year with the exception of one game. In our opener, he came off the bench and tossed in 14 points in a key role against Lakewood Community College. I felt he deserved a start and in our next game at Gogebic C.C. in Michigan's Upper Peninsula. I gave him his chance. Well, he was so nervous and shook up his play turned out terrible. He threw several interceptions, traveled a couple of times, and Gogebic raced to a quick 12 point lead. After a hasty timeout, I took hold of his jersey and asked him, "What color is your jersey?" He replied in a somewhat shaky voice, "Red." Then in a sarcastic tone of voice, I came back at him with, "Then throw the ball to a player wearing a red jersey." (Gogebic was wearing white). I decided Doug would be more productive coming off the bench and that's what he did for the remainder of the year.

Another Schmitz experience in college basketball also occurred in the Upper Peninsula of Michigan as we battled Suomi College. Suomi

Richard W. Varichak

had a 5'10" guard named Tom Johnson, who was a scoring machine. Doug had the unfortunate task of defending him. On a fast break by Suomi with Johnson handling the ball, Doug and Tom Ronchetti dropped back on defense to the free throw line to double team Johnson on his drive to the bucket. Satisfied that they had the path to the basket blocked, both Schmitz and Ronchetti were amazed to see Johnson take off from the free throw line, soaring over their hands to dunk the ball. I wouldn't have believed it if I didn't see the feat for myself. What a remarkable play!! We didn't win that game either. Doug muttered, "All I saw were his tenners flying over my head."

As a sophomore Doug became a team leader and a coach on the floor. Although the season was a disappointment in wins and losses, the relationship I had with the players was satisfying and fulfilling. Wade Olson and Doug went on to become teachers and coaches, Bob Eggers graduated with a degree in engineering, and Rick Stark attained his dental degree.

Doug was also one of my better baseball players and he was very instrumental in helping me get baseball in our athletic program. In that first year we had to play club baseball. The school would not fund our program until they felt it would be successful. The first year we borrowed uniforms from the city team. The umpires, led by Babe Glumack, worked free of charge. We drove our own autos to road games. The schools with established programs fit us into their schedule. Like most beginning programs, we had some good baseball players (Schmitz, Marty Trenberth, Dario Rolle) but very little in the pitching department. We did get the services of John Anderson from Nashwauk-Keewatin and he did a fine job when he was on the mound. But when we had to go to "throwers" we were in trouble. John transferred to the University of Minnesota where he played and now is the Gopher head coach and is in the Community College Hall of Fame, along with Doug. It was Doug who once again led the team in most offensive slots and was a coach on the field. He helped set up our annual spring baseball trips to Texas and when he took over head job, made arrangements to fly the team to Florida for our "spring training." The move from Austin, Texas became necessary

Fifty-Five Years on the Bench

because we were having too many games cancelled because of rain and inclement weather that hit the city for a couple years. But I think Doug wanted to fly and see Florida. Regardless, it was a good move and the kids really enjoyed the trips.

On one of our trips to Austin, Texas we had a chance to play in Disch-Falk baseball stadium, the home field of the University of Texas Longhorns. Cliff Gustafson, the Longhorn coach, had assembled some of his freshman players who didn't get much varsity action to play us. Cliff wanted to know if he could pitch a sophomore who was recovering from a sore arm, but also warned us he was a varsity player. Doug agreed to let him pitch and the kids found out what a major league pitcher can do. The sore-armed pitcher was Roger Clemens who went on to gain All-American honors as a Texas Longhorn and of course, developed as one of the top pitchers in Major League Baseball. Incidentally, we lost the game 27-2 but Ken Henning our center fielder nicked Clemens for our two hits.

Doug closed out his community college baseball coaching career with a Minnesota State Community College Championship. He was an excellent recruiter who did not only recruit bodies, but athletes who fit in his program. The great strength he possessed was his ability to teach athletes their respective positions while not playing those positions himself. During his stint as a basketball coach, he took the low post players, the big guys and girls, and made them betters players at their

Figure 17: Photo by Carole Lind - PIO from Hibbing CC.
Head Coach Doug Schmitz and Assistant Coach Dick Varichak take time out from practice with their HCC Cagers.

Richard W. Varichak

positions. He took Rob Schoenrock, a good low post player from Hinckley and made him into a top notch college center. Rob was able to go on and play for the Minnesota Gophers in his last two years. All this teaching from a pint-sized guard! With the baseball program, although he was not a pitcher, he was responsible for developing a strong, disciplined pitching staff. This good pitching enabled his team to be a constant championship caliber club each year.

Doug has a type "A" personality. He is quick to get agitated when the team plays badly. But he also is quick to praise a player's performance when the team prospers because of the player's contribution. He is a consummate bench coach. Nobody outcoaches him in game strategy although sometimes he outcoaches himself. He is an official's dream coach. He respects officials and very seldom does he get on them, although I do remember one incident when he and I were coaching the men's Cardinal basketball team. We were at home against a tough Vermilion Community College team and the officiating became a little inconsistent. One of the officials was past his prime and shouldn't have been officiating college ball. He was too slow and out of position for most of the game. I could see Doug was getting more and more irritated as the game progressed. The older official was not one of Doug's favorites and they had words in the past. Finally that Schmitz temper got the best of him and he had some choice words after a terrible call. The official was quick to give him a "T" (technical foul) and I hurriedly dragged him back to the bench before he got another one. I was too late! Coming off the floor he made another suggestive remark to the referee and, sure enough, he was tagged with "T" number two. Under game rule this meant automatic ejection from the gym. So, I was left to coach the team for the remainder of the game. The situation was Vermilion 48, Hibbing 45 with ten minutes left to play. Before Doug left the floor he told me he would sit on the stairs outside the locker room. I was to send one of our reserves back to him and he would send in directions through the sub to help me out. After a couple of trips by our sub and suggestions from Doug, I thought, "Wait a minute! I've been a basketball coach for many years and why should a younger coach sitting on steps

Fifty-Five Years on the Bench

give me strategy!" So I told the young lad, running back and forth to Doug, "Keep your seat, because I can make decisions." I slipped into the role of head coach and for the next seven minutes traded strategy with Paul McDonald, the Vermilion mentor. As the game went on we slowly took the lead and ended up winning by ten points. I really didn't have anything to do with the win- the kids just realized that I knew what I was doing and they responded. Doug's comment after the game, "Maybe I should get kicked out more often."

After 20 years at Hibbing Community College, without being hired as a full time faculty instructor, Doug moved over to Nashwauk-Keewatin High School. He became the Spartans head boys' basketball coach and Athletic Director. I thought I was having a lot of fun coaching with him, so I followed him over to be an assistant. We were joined by Dick Larson, the ex-Hibbing Bluejacket coach, giving our staff a ton of basketball coaching experience. The boys' program had been down for the past three years, winning only twelve games against 56 losses. In the next three years the team carved out 45 wins and 25 losses, plus winning two conference championships and finishing second place once. We coaches had a ball in those three years and basically enjoyed most of the boys. Of course, we met a couple of parents who felt their sons were not getting enough playing time or had their feelings hurt when the coaches had to correct or discipline them. This happens more often on the high school level- something we didn't experience in the college program.

Doug was let go after his third year, with the reason being a drop in enrollment. My belief is that the administration was pushed into letting him go. The school lost a dedicated teacher and coach because of some petty behavior. However, he was now on his way to eight great years at Hibbing High School and the girls' program.

First, though, he took a teaching and coaching job with Mora High School, about 120 miles south of Hibbing. Kathy and their girls remained in Hibbing, so Doug lived in Mora for five days, coming home to Hibbing on weekends. After a year of this commuting, the Schmitz family decided it wasn't worth all the traveling and being separated from each other. Doug was fortunate in obtaining a position with the Mesabi

Trail Organization, a job which he still holds today and thoroughly enjoys. Meanwhile, when Doug was in Mora, I got drafted by my granddaughter, Shawna, to coach her eighth grade team. Dave Ongaro shared coaching duties and that was the beginning of my eight-year tenure with the Hibbing girls' program. The next year I was appointed assistant varsity coach and Shawna became a starter as a 9th grader with the varsity squad. My other granddaughter, Lindsay, and Doug's daughter, Jodi, were in 7th grade and were part of their basketball program. Lindsay persuaded me to coach their team and I agreed, knowing that I would be coaching two teams and two granddaughters. Knowing Doug was in Hibbing now, and not coaching anywhere, I asked him to help and he readily agreed. I considered us co-coaches, and we started another great coaching relationship. This seventh grade team was to give us the experience that all coaches look forward to and relish. My varsity coaching duties lasted for only one year under Coach Clusiau as I chose to give all my attention to our 7th graders.

We had 18 girls on our seventh grade squad, so we divided the team into a blue group and a white group. Doug and I took the blue team, who consisted of our top seven players, while Coach Brian Karich took the white team. We recognized the athleticism and intelligence of our seven players and started teaching them the advanced skills which we felt they could master. Other coaches did not think that the girls, as young as they were, would be able to handle those advanced skills. We put in a full court press, a half-court press, emphasized a sticky man-to-man defense and threw in a zone coverage to give the girls something different. We gave them a simple offense and this was enough because we discovered that many of our scores came off our defense with steals and violations we caused. Our Blue team finished the season with a 27-3 record, our three losses coming to AAU combinations in St. Cloud and Rochester. More to come about our "Fab Nine" in chapter nine.

Doug finally got the head girls basketball job in 2003 and that was the start of the change in Bluejacket fortunes. He also wanted me to be on his staff and I readily agreed. We had to leave our "fab nine" for a year as they would now be playing C-team ball while tackling freshman

Fifty-Five Years on the Bench

academics. The Bluejackets had gone through a few years of trying to find some wins, usually not winning over seven games a season the past three years. One change we introduced was to have the varsity and junior varsity practice together, and then a year later we included the C-team. We wanted the three programs all under our practice routine and we felt it worked out to our and the players' satisfaction.

We had to break a lot of bad basketball habits and convince the girls to buy into our philosophy. Most of the girls responded to our program changes and the players who found it too difficult to adjust dropped out fairly quickly. We were run out of the gym in our opener against Greenway but managed to run up a 12-12 record, the most wins attained in the past four years. We had some fine assistant coaches who proved to be pretty good teachers. Kaye Anderson handled our Jr. Varsity; Jeff Jacobson worked with us on the varsity while Randy Williamson and Anne Swanson directed our C-team. Greg Helstrom took over the Jr. Varsity when Anderson retired and enjoyed winning seasons each year he headed the club. His approach to the game and his work ethic led to his selection as head coach when Doug called it quits. I retired the year before on my 55th year of coaching and was ready to be just a spectator. Doug saved a place on the bench for me but I reminded him that I did not want to be involved in the game. My participation to date is to accompany the girls on road trips to keep the scorebook.

Anna Matetich, one of our top notch players who finished in 2006, had some difficulty in adjusting in her sophomore year. She said, "I remember at first struggling to buy into their system. Dick and Doug didn't mess around. They ran their practices like nothing I had ever seen before. It took us awhile, but as we gradually bought into it we saw better results. Once we got over that hump there was really no looking back. Our program was really in shambles before they came along and they were exactly what we needed. They turned us into a very disciplined team where everyone contributed and pushed for improvement. Coach V. was one nobody wanted to disappoint."

Matetich turned out to be one of the finest ball players in our program and led the Jackets to a 26-2 season record and a runner-up spot

Richard W. Varichak

in section play in her senior year. She was a prime example why coaching is so much fun and fulfilling.

Our "fab nine" finally became seniors in the school year 2006-2007. All nine of them stuck with the program and all lettered throughout their high school careers. When they were blowing everyone off the floor in 7th and 8th grade I mentioned to them after one of our games, "You nine players will take us to the State Tournament when you are varsity players." They made that prediction come true in their senior year. The team finished with a 24-5 record and defeated Duluth East in the Section 7 Tournament to qualify for the State. It was all the more enjoyable by winning the section crown in the Hibbing Memorial Building in front of our home fans.

We had the misfortune to meet a tough DeLaSalle team in our State Tourney opener. They were just too quick and tough on the boards and eliminated us 50-37. But Lindsay Jacobson, Jodi Schmitz, Nikki Klinck, Nicole Nyberg, Stacy Burdick, Kelly Manney, Hannah Miesbauer, Stevie Pelkey, and Amber Brant will always play a huge part in our coaching life.

Doug Schmitz has proven himself to be an excellent teacher and coach. He has turned programs around no matter where he has coached. At Hibbing Community College he took both the men's basketball and baseball teams to greater heights than they had experienced in the preceding dozen years before he took the reins. With the Nashwauk-Keewatin Spartan boys he carved out a 45-25 record and two Conference Championships in the next three years. The Hibbing Bluejackets, who couldn't win more than 7 games per year in recent years, used the Schmitz-Varichak magic to attain a 125-42 won-loss record with four Iron Range Championships and a Section 7 crown. He

Figure 18: Photo by Larry Ryan
Schmitz Family
Front: Doug & Kathy
Back: Jodi, Kate, Julie

Fifty-Five Years on the Bench

was tough to beat as a bench coach and I have never seen a coach who prepared a team as well as he does. I truly believe he knew our opponents as well or better than their own coach. He can be tough on his players and he was even tough on Jodi, his daughter. There were times where

Figure 19: Photo by Al Higgins, Hibbing CC
Coaches Doug Schmitz and Dick Varichak go over half-time strategy with HCC Cardinals – 1995.

I had to soothe her hurt feelings after she and her dad had a disagreement. But like Jodi, who knew her dad loved her, Doug also felt this love for all his players, even though they drew his ire with some negative action. He and I had disagreements over the years but he always listened to my side and never held it against me when I lost my temper and gave him a piece of my mind. His respect for me was totally honest and I was very grateful that disagreements (sometimes heated) did not interfere with our close relationship. He stressed execution and expected his players to improve this execution to the best of their ability. He could easily forgive physical errors but abhorred mental miscues. At times he could get somewhat abrasive with players during games, but he never lost his affections for those who played for him.

Richard W. Varichak

I will miss working with him and I hope he can find some more coaching opportunities because he has so much to contribute to athletics. It's been a great ride for the Schmitz-Varichak era and we humbly thank the many hundreds of student-athletes who blessed our lives.

Chapter 7: Hibbing Cardinal Cagers – Basketball Can Be So Much Fun

After spending three years guiding high school girls' basketball teams in Texas, I began directing college men at Hibbing Junior College in 1963. The year spent at Darrouzett High School was enjoyable giving me added experience at the coaching level and administration as a high school principal. I was ready to spend another year there because I was rehired as girls' basketball coach and principal. But then I received a call from Joe Milinovich, my coach whom I played for at Hibbing J.C. in 1950-51.

He caught me one Saturday morning grading some biology tests. He asked me how far I was from Amarillo and I told him about 75 miles. He told me the Cardinals had won their way to the National Junior College basketball tournament in Hutchinson, Kansas. His first opponent was going to be either San Angelo or Amarillo J.C. who were in a one game playoff. He asked me to scout the game and then invited Noka and me up to Hutchinson to see the National Tourney game. I took a vacation day on a Wednesday and Noka and I drove to Hutchinson, which believe it or not, was only 140 miles from Darrouzett, even though we traveled in three states!

We saw an exciting over-time game in which Hibbing prevailed by two points. Joe invited us to have a post-game meal with the team and we gratefully accepted. During the meal, he worked trying to convince Noka that Hibbing was the "dream spot" in Minnesota. At this point I realized Joe was offering me a job. He was moving from the physical education department to teach history the next year and was giving up the head basketball and track posts. Of course his offer had to be officially certified by Doctor Hudnall, the college dean, but he assured me that the dean was in agreement with Joe. That darn Joe had already had me picked before he got to Hutchinson!! What a guy!

In a couple of days I received a call from Dr. Hudnall offering me the job with a $1,500 raise in pay. I accepted with mounting excite-

Fifty-Five Years on the Bench

ment, because I felt this was a move upward in the educational field and I was glad to be coming home. I left Darrouzett with many positive feelings and some close friends, both adults and student-athletes. This also would be a new experience for Noka and my two children, Tom and Vikki, who were ten and seven years of age. Tom would enter the fifth grade and Vikki would start on her educational ladder in first grade, both at Greenhaven Elementary.

Joe Milinovich didn't wait long to put me to work as he convinced me I would get to know the kids quicker if I came aboard as a volunteer assistant football coach. I didn't get to do much coaching because I found out Joe was a hands on coach. He ran everything from offense to defense and the special teams, involving the kick-off and punting teams. Terry Carlson from our math department was the full-time assistant and was mainly responsible to fill in places where Joe either forgot or didn't have time to attend. Terry was a competent coach, and he and Joe complemented each other in their coaching responsibilities. So I just stood around, took care of dirty practice gear and, fortunately learned more about the game of football. Joe was an excellent football coach and was still teaching me, some thirteen years after I was a Cardinal football player.

Figure 20: Arnie Maki - Hibbing Junior College
Donald James Stahl
1943 - 2012
Cardinal All-American for HCC in 1964. One of the great shooters in Cardinal basketball history and a successful coach and teacher.

The season which I was waiting for was college basketball! Last year's team graduated all the big men- only the half pints would be back to carry us into the basketball wars. However, two starters were back and they proved to be our two top scorers and team leaders. Don Stahl, a Chisholm graduate was a shooting sensation. He stood 6'0" and was slow

Richard W. Varichak

a foot, but could he shoot! His range of shots measured between a two foot layup to a 40 foot-long heave which continually hit nothing but net. His running mate was Bill Skarich, an all-around student athlete from Keewatin. Bill was only 5'10" but was an outstanding outside shooter. He proved to be a triple threat because his quickness enabled him to continually drive to the basket, drawing a multitude of free throws. Not only was he an accurate shooter from the field, but he was equally deadly from the free throw line. These two sophomores were my building blocks and I added Bob Sinko from Chisholm, Pete Kinney from Hibbing, and George "Butch" Varichak from Renton, Washington. If George's last name is the same as mine that would be because he is my younger brother, who at the age of 24 decided to go to college. I kind of "recruited" him in the summer of 1963 when my family spent three months with my parents in Renton. George had decided to go to college when he found what my Masters Degree could do when Boeing Aircraft offered me a job within ten minutes of my application for summer work.

Those five players were to be my starters for the season of 1963-64 with three players at 5'10", one at 5'11" and one at 6'0". People thought I was crazy. After all, I had Ed Pessenda at 6'4", Dan Hyduke at 6'3", and Darnell Blume at 6'5" on the bench. Through the pre-season practices and scrimmages, the midget size players I had started were the best combination in our "run and gun" offense and pressing defenses. I got a big kick out of watching opposing teams during our warm-ups licking their lips in preparing to decimate our vertically challenged five. But it wasn't long before our opponents found themselves on the short end of the score early in the game and many of our contests were over at half-time. Stahl, Skarich, Kinney, and Sinko bombarded opponents with their outside fire power, while George, although only 5'11", was tough on the boards and cleaned up on the missed shots to throw in his 7- 10 points per game.

Not only did we average 94 points a game, and remember this was before the 3-point shot, but we went 17-4 and won the conference championship. The Region 13 Tourney was held in the Hibbing Memorial Building, thus giving us somewhat of a home court advantage. Then I

Fifty-Five Years on the Bench

observed our first opponent on opening night, the big talented Austin Bluedevils. Their size wore us down in the first half and we trailed 53-36 at the intermission. But then something remarkable happened. In my coaching career I never saw such an incredible second half comeback as our Cardinals achieved that night. With the little guys shooting the lights out of the gym and George out-rebounding his bigger foes, Hibbing came back to win 91-90. The team set a field goal record by sinking 24 out of 27 attempts. The ending of the game was the most dramatic part of the contest. Bill Skarich stepped to the free throw line with the score 89-90 in Austin's favor and five seconds left in the game. Skarich netted both throws to put Hibbing one point ahead. Austin took the throw-in to midcourt and called timeout. Only two seconds left – the ball was thrown in to one of their high scoring guards who let go a desperation-shot from the half court line that swished through the hoop. The basket was waived off by the officials because the horn ending the game had sounded while the shooter had the ball in his hands. Needless to say, I was one limp and worn-out coach at that time.

Unfortunately, the next evening, we met a bigger, faster team from Willmar Junior College who knocked us out of the competition in an eight point loss. We just couldn't handle their size and Willmar went on to win the tournament and advanced to the National playoffs. We had to be satisfied with a third place finish as we spanked Virginia J.C. in a lackluster game.

My first college team at Hibbing proved to be one of the finest clubs in my coaching experience. My big problem for next year was how were we going to duplicate the success we enjoyed in the past season?

It didn't take long before we knocked on the championship door again. After a couple of second place finishes I found six players that put together some great chemistry and over-achieved their way to a conference championship in 1968. These six players headed by sophomore captain Greg Crnkovich were joined by freshmen Bill Zeiher from Hibbing, Greg Grcevich from Nashwauk-Keewatin, Jim Miskulin and

Richard W. Varichak

Tom Butorac ex-Chisholm Bluestreaks, and Mark Maki from Buhl. Although not a very deep club, they battled their way to a 12-2 conference crown. Some of our wins were ugly but they got the job done and the big thing I had to worry about was hoping the studs would stay away from fouling out.

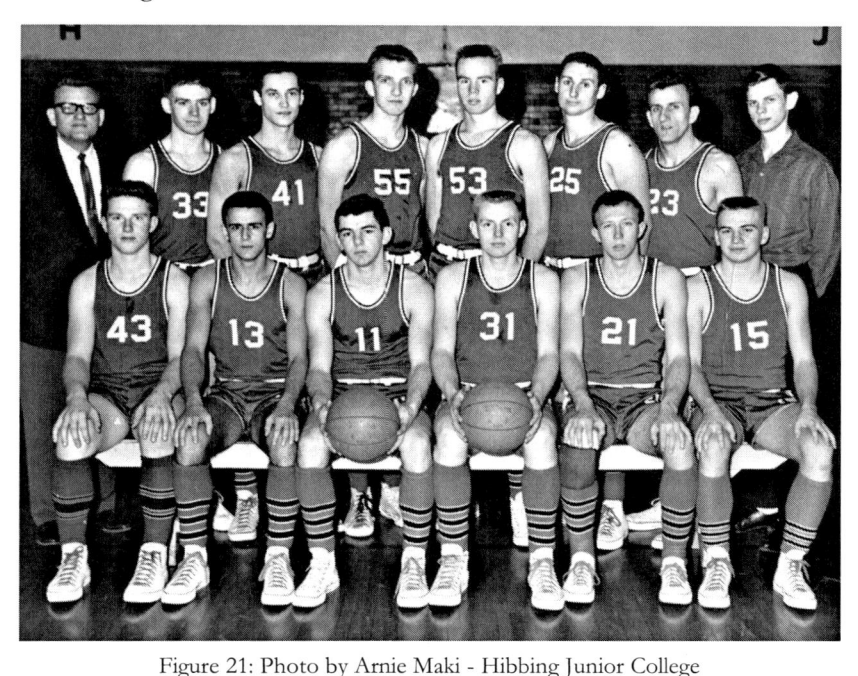

Figure 21: Photo by Arnie Maki - Hibbing Junior College
1963-64 HJC Cardinals – 17 wins, 4 losses
Northern Junior College Conference Champions
Region 13 Tournament Consolation Winners
Back row: Coach Dick Varichak, Tim Gillis, Dan Hyduke, Ed Pessenda, Darnell Blume, Bob Perfetti, George Varichak, Jon Timpane. Front row: Clyde Morse, Bob Sinko, Bill Skarich, Don Stahl, Pete Kinney, Dick Johnson

Fifty-Five Years on the Bench

Figure 22: Photo by Al Higgins – Hibbing State Junior College
1968-69 HSJC Basketball Team
Highest scoring HCC team with 101.6 points per game, 18 wins, 6 losses.
Top row: Tom White, Merty Hirt, Roger Rossman, Ken Lee, Greg Grcevich, Roger Koskela, Frank Russ, Bill Zeiher, Tom Tintor, Coach Dick Varichak. Front row: Jim Miskulin, Tom Butorac, Greg Violette, Mike Anselmo, Bob Edelstein.

With Grcevich, Butorac, Miskulin, and Zeiher returning the next year, these four became the building blocks who formed the highest scoring team in Cardinal basketball history. We were fortunate in recruiting high school All-American Frank Russ, Tom Tintor and Kenny Lee from Hibbing's District Champions, and those seven provided fire power that most opponents could not match. In fact, Miskulin and Butorac, who were starters the year before, had to come off the bench. But in my mind, this gave us seven starters. Also Mirty Hirt and Bob Edelstein from the Hibbing Bluejacket program gave us added strength off the bench. We were 22-6, playing a tough schedule, losing a pair of games to a four year college in Canada. We averaged 101.8 points a game, going over the century mark ten times. We set a state scoring record by defeating Lakewood Community College 156-96.

One of the high points of the season when we played in Thunder Bay, Canada at Lakehead University in a weekend double header. Frank Russ, our leading scorer, was averaging close to 30 points a contest and

Richard W. Varichak

was receiving a lot of media coverage. This was not lost on the Lakehead team and they were prepared to cut this All-American down to size. On the first night, Frank faced double and triple team coverage and had one of his lowest scoring games, netting only 15 points in an 84-76 loss. He took some brickbats and negative remarks from some of the fans and I could see Frank was bothered. He was unusually quiet for the remainder of the evening but the next afternoon during the warm-up period, I could see a steady resolve in his eyes. Boy! – did he go to work! When we had a 27-24 lead in the first half, Frank had 24 of those points. He did it in all kinds of moves – set shot, tip-in, drive-in, hook shot, and was putting on a scoring show. We did get edged again, 84-81 but Frank tallied 32 points, even though he missed the last five minutes of the game with five fouls. He left the game to a standing ovation from the crowd, who had been so critical of him the night before. Frank made us all proud that day.

Although this was one of my favorite teams, health setbacks kept us from going as far as I thought we would. In the playoff game to go to the Nationals, we faced Gogebic in our gym and I was pretty confident of a win. However, just a few days before the game, both of my guards, Kenny Lee and Tom Butorac came down with hepatitis and could not play. With the loss of these two important cogs and inspired play by Gogebic, the visitors upset us 83-82 on a last second basket. One of my low points on the coaching scale. What a disappointment!

I left Hibbing that next year to attend the University of Wyoming to work on a PhD on a two year sabbatical leave. Frank and Greg Grcevich transferred to University of Denver where both of them played on the Pioneer Team. Bill Zeiher received a full ride at Florida Institute of Technology where he played for two more years and captained the team in his senior year. Bill graduated with an Electrical Engineering degree and went to work with the CIA. Russ later transferred to UMD where he sparked the Duluth club for two years, received his B.S. degree in Physical Education, and taught at Hermantown for many years. Grcevich attained his business degree and became a successful insurance tycoon in the Twin Cities. My two ex-Bluestreaks, Tom Butorac received

Fifty-Five Years on the Bench

his law degree, and Jim Miskulin attained his nursing degree. I often wondered what the outcome would be if my 1964 team played my 1969 club. I know there would be a bushel-full of points.

I returned to Hibbing after one year at Wyoming – came a paper short of getting the PhD and the family (especially son, Tom) was eager to get back to Northern Minnesota. I inherited a top-notch player, Dave Homoky from Merriville, Indiana, but I will elaborate on him in a later chapter. After enjoying a team that averaged 101 points a game earlier, my 1971 team had difficulty scoring. Bob Loushine from Chisholm and Tom Vucetich from Hibbing had most of the point totals. But things brightened the next year when I got the services of Doug Schmitz from Sebeka, Bob Eggers, Rick Stark, and Wade Olson from Hibbing, along with Tom Gornick and Lou Janezich from Chisholm.

We did a creditable job in their freshman year, but it was the strangest season the next year when they were sophomores. With a veteran team composed mainly of good student athletes we went 6-16. The weirdest part of the season was losing 10 of those 16 losses either in the last minute or second or overtimes. As the season progressed, I could see in the players' eyes, "How are we going to lose tonight?" For the first time in my coaching career I felt I wasn't doing my job. With the exception of losing good kids like Schmitz, Eggers, Gornick, Olson, and Janezich, I was glad to see the season end.

After being away from girls' basketball for the past 29 years, I was inadvertently pushed back into the role of head coach for the 1991-1992 Cardinal women. Actually our football coach, Dale Heffron, was assigned the job, but left the college after the football season ended. Provost Orville Olson asked me if I would take the position and I accepted. My problem was that the assignment to coach the girls put me over a full teaching load and the administration was not too keen on paying overload pay. I solved the problem by hiring my daughter-in-law, Tammy and I would coach for nothing. The story of my life!

Once again, I was faced with a shortage of players. Girls' basketball at Hibbing Community College had not drawn many candidates in the past few years. Tammy had been one of the better players in the 80's

Richard W. Varichak

and was now an elementary teacher at Jefferson Elementary School. We ended up with six full-time players and several who joined the team but then quit after a few days. All six girls were freshmen, so I thought it would be a long year with a lot of teaching involved. The team was led by a couple of sharp shooters who had led their respective high schools in scoring. Char Omdahl from Mesabi East and Julie Wickstrom from Barnum would end up as our top scorers. Two ex-Hibbing Bluejacket cagers, Lisa Caldwell and Becky Koslowski, gave us blue collar efforts with their strong physical play and defense. Gina Quirk from Chisholm contributed to our low post attack while Michel Dicklich, a pint-sized guard from Northwestern H.S. in Wisconsin, provided long range shooting. Dicklich came off the bench most of the time and could replace any of the starters. If she replaced Quirk at center, we would move Caldwell over to the post, so we were always making adjustment. To be able to practice against competition, I recruited several of the male athletes to provide opposition. This worked out fine, because the boys played their parts without over-powering the girls.

The girls were all heart during the season, but their grit really came out in our last game of the year at Mesabi Community College. We had a close game earlier in Hibbing, with Mesabi edging us 49-45. This one was also a cliffhanger, only it was Hibbing hanging by our finger-nails. With three minutes left and the Cardinals leading 48-45, I lost my third player to 5 fouls ejection. Now that left me with three players to battle Mesabi's five, so that three point lead started to disappear. I had to put my girls in a triangle zone defense and they played with determination I had never seen before. But five against three wore us out and Mesabi finally prevailed 53-48. I was never as proud of my gals as I was at that moment. The two officials, Tom Vucetich and Tim Scott, had played for me back in the day, Vucetich in basketball and Scott in baseball. They sure didn't take it easy on the Ole Coach with their whistle blowing. Actually they did a pretty good job that night.

Although our record was only 6-15, we beat Itasca three times, but lost several over-time games- we just ran out of gas each time. This group of girls gave me more satisfaction and coaching enjoyment than

Fifty-Five Years on the Bench

many of my more successful teams. As I do with my 1960-61 girls' team in Evant, Texas, I have kept in close contact with the five remaining players from this Hibbing squad. Sadly, Becky Koslowski was killed in an auto accident and I miss her and her eye-catching smile.

This was when we hired Doug Schmitz. Doug had graduated from the University of Minnesota, got married and was looking for a job. His wife, Kathy was hired to teach at Washington Elementary in Hibbing, so this was my chance to get Doug back into our coaching family. He served as my assistant in both basketball and baseball. I then handed the reins over to him in both sports and he became one of the youngest head coaches at age 24. He immediately showed that he was a top-notch coach and brought both our basketball and baseball programs to a high level.

Figure 23: Photo by Al Higgins - Hibbing Community College
Don Varichak – Cardinal Sharp Shooter, with Coaches Dick Varichak and Doug Schmitz

I was fortunate to team up with Doug the year I retired in 1992. He asked me to be his basketball assistant and for the next five years, we had a successful run at Minnesota Community College honors. The highlight of those years centered on the two championship years in 1993-1995. It was one of those times when a group of outstanding athletes decided to come to our school. We were glad to get Hibbing Bluejacket aces, Nick Theising, Spinner Aune, Rob Bigelow, and Jeremey Fleming. Our front line was blessed with the addition of 6'7" Rob Schoenrock from Hinckley-Finlayson and 6'6" Matt Swanson from Duluth East. A pleasant surprise was the enrollment of Jim Brewer, a 6'3" sharp shooter

Richard W. Varichak

from East St. Louis. Mark Cool from Cloquet and Jeff Buffetta from Mt. Iron- Buhl gave us valuable additional guard strength.

The second year of the Theising- led Cardinals we went to the championship game in the State Tournament. Our opponent was a nationally ranked Minneapolis Community College team who had defeated us earlier in the year. The game proved to be one of those down to the wire contests, but Minneapolis had too many guns and tripped us up by ten points. One of the big moments for us and Jim Brewer came in the semi-final game with Willmar the night before. With Hibbing trailing by one point, Jim sank a corner jumper with five seconds left to give us the one point win and the trip to the finals. The other big moment came when it was announced before the game that Coach Schmitz had been selected as Coach of the Year! This was a well deserved honor for our young Cardinal Coach.

The final years of my coaching association with Hibbing C.C. along with Doug, came the next two seasons when we had to do without Theising, Aune, Schoenrock, Swanson, and Brewer. The cupboard didn't stay bare very long with the addition of several talented recruits. Heading this list was Cory Schlagel, an all-around player from Rush City, Jim Johnson, a 6 '7 center out of Duluth Central, and Jim Milkovich, a 6 '9 pivot from the Hibbing Bluejackets. Those three talented players went on to play four year ball after graduation from Hibbing. Schlagel was one of the finest players to enter our coaching life. A great student, a very talented basketball player, and a super individual, we knew he would go far. He went on to St. Thomas University where he played two more years, received his math degree and now teaches and coaches at Albany High School. He also helps his Uncle Kevin with the St. Cloud University men's basketball team.

Johnson continued his basketball action at Moorhead State University where he received his business degree. Milkovich transferred to North Dakota University but did not play any more basketball. He attained a degree in electrical engineering, concluding a fine academic career.

Fifty-Five Years on the Bench

So after 34 years at Hibbing Community College, with 19 of them involved in basketball, I feel blessed to have one of the best jobs I ever had. Hibbing Community College, especially the basketball part, will always be a highlight experience in my professional life. Thank you, Joe Milinovich!

Figure 24: Photo by Carole Lind - Hibbing Community College
Minnesota Community College Hall of Fame
1992 Inductees
Frank Russ, Don Stahl, and Coach Dick Varichak

Chapter 8: Athletes Can Produce the Strangest Sitcoms

If one coaches long enough, one may be subject to some of the strangest, probably comical, and certainly different than the normal happenings. In my fifty-five years of coaching experience, I had the fortune, or misfortune, of being involved in several cases of "Oh boy! What happened?"

I hadn't donned my coaching shoes very long when the first of my bizarre incidents came about in my first year on a basketball court. With my Evant boys' basketball team, we were in action against Bertram High School, on their court. We had a commanding lead and our big scorer that night was Clynton Smith, our 6'2", 250-pound forward. I heard their coach telling one of his players who was about to go into the game, "Get that number 52 (Smith)." As Clynton came down the floor near the scoring table, the Bertram sub hauled off and punched Clynton in the nose, knocking him down. The sub looked over to his coach and asked, "OK, Coach?" Needless to say, their coach had buried his head in his hands and was on his knees. The referee stopped the game, called a technical foul on the player and ejected him from the game. Clynton's comment – "I got hit harder on the football field."

Once again, in Evant, during a basketball game in which we were heavily favored, I faced another unusual incident. Before the game, one of the officials, who was a good friend to both Noka and me, asked if he could call a technical foul on my wife if we had the contest well in hand. Noka can be a little vociferous at games and will let officials know how wrong they are on occasion. Sure enough as we raced to a 35 point lead, she let out with one of her "uncomplimentary" suggestions on the officiating. The official slowly walked up to where she was sitting, looked her square in the eye, and said, "Oh hell, I can't do it" and burst out laughing as we all did.

Moving forward to Hibbing High School gym #2, during one of our junior high girls' games, I was witness to one of the more entertaining pieces of basketball. Late in the game, a shot attempt by a Mesabi

Fifty-Five Years on the Bench

East player was rebounded by our player who lost it out-of-bounds. Their player in-bounded the ball which was intercepted by one of our girls. In her confusion, she immediately shot at Mesabi East's basket. Fortunately, she missed the shot but captured the rebound- and took another shot! This shot also missed while her teammates and coach were screaming at her for shooting at the wrong basket. She picked off her second missed shot and as she was attempting a third straight shot, a teammate fouled her in an attempt to block the shot. The two young officials looked at me after stopping play and asked, "Coach, what do we call?" I was as mystified as they were about the call. I thought, "You can't give our girl two free throws – she was shooting at Mesabi East's basket." After a minute, I offered, "Rule a violation against Hibbing and give the ball to Mesabi East." That seemed to satisfy both teams, except our young shooter, who will probably remember her gaffe for the rest of her life.

Did you ever see a scuffle on the court during play – between your own players? I never had this happen to me before, or after, this crazy incident. My Hibbing Junior College team was in Thief River Falls, Minnesota in 1966, battling the Northland Junior College five. During a missed shot by Northland, a scuffle broke out under the basket and involved my two best scorers, Greg Crnkovich and Ed Tekautz. As they pushed each other around – well, let Crnkovich tell it in his own words:

"During this game, Ed Tekautz and I got into a confrontation about who was going to cover whom on defense and he pushed me towards one of the players on the opposite team, which I thought was an aggressive manner, so I pushed him back. This behavior continued for several minutes. Then Coach Varichak called a time out and began verbally chewing us out during the time out. Coach Varichak was so mad at us that he took his shoe off and threw it in the bleachers behind us. After this, things calmed down, but our behavior probably cost us the game."

My action, after I retrieved my shoe, was to bench both players, which meant sitting my two top scorers. I also didn't start them in the next game the following afternoon. Ed Tekautz, many years later, met me

Richard W. Varichak

in a grocery store. He brought the incident up and believe it or not, offered an apology for his actions that night. Well, better late than never, I say.

Another time my Hibbing Cardinals made headlines through a sports photograph. We were playing Bismarck Junior College from North Dakota in Region 13 playoffs to qualify for a National Tourney berth. With a few minutes left in the game, Ron Margo, our captain, drove in for a shot, got undercut, and fell to the floor knocked unconscious. Time out was taken and I raced onto the court, dreading the worst. The Bismarck Coach motioned his players over to their bench. Not only did his players come over, so did one of mine. Pepperpot guard, Joe Davich, joined the Bismarck huddle, much to the amazement of their coach and players. Well, I'll let Joe tell it as it happened.

"During the next chaotic moments, medical attention was given to Ron, causing a long delay. The Bismarck Coach decided to call his players over for an unauthorized time out. As I watched the Bismarck players gather, I was determined not to allow the flagrant foul become an advantage for them. So, I boldly walked into the Bismarck team huddle and stood facing the coach among his players (this time out was not official and as a player, I was allowed to be anywhere on the court.) The Bismarck Coach and players were stunned that I had the audacity to step in amongst them despite being pushed and elbowed by some of the players. Finally, an exasperated coach, realizing that he was not going to be able to provide any strategy, just sat down. As it turned out, a Willmar newspaper photographer snapped a picture of me in the huddle and sent the picture and caption to all the national news wires. Weeks later, I received copies of the picture from Iron Rangers who were living throughout the United States."

Fifty-Five Years on the Bench

I completely missed Joe's action as I was concerned with Ron who by that time had regained consciousness. My only knowledge of his invasion of the huddle was through the picture. What a fighter Joe turned out to be!

What's So Funny About This Picture

Figure 25: Photo by Willmar Tribune

I don't know if you can see the people in the background laughing about the scene above, but something is radically wrong with the picture above taken during a time out in the Bismarck-Hibbing game. Have you spotted it?
It seems like Joe Davich, on the far left from Hibbing, enjoyed the talk being given by Bismarck coach, Bob Johnson, more than he liked what was going on around his bench. He didn't learn enough though as Bismarck squeaked out a last second win. No. 30 for Bismarck is "Pepsi" Freeman, No. 24 is Don McDaniel and No. 54 is Dave Lawson.

I've seen coaches accosted by irate fans and/or parents after games, but I had the opportunity to get chewed out in the second quarter of a junior high girls' contest. Our 8th grade Hibbing girls were on the

Richard W. Varichak

road playing at Greenway. It was a mismatch from the opening tip-off. Our girls were the powerhouse of Northeast Minnesota and Greenway was in the midst of poor basketball talent. We normally throw a full-court press to open the game and it unnerved the Coleraine team as we raced to a 21-1 lead at the end of the first quarter. We pulled the press off and stayed with our sticky man-to-man defense. This change in our defense was also devastating to the Greenway attack and pretty soon we upped the lead to 34-3. At this point, one of the Greenway mothers walked across the floor (the teams were battling at one end of the court), pointed her finger in my face and screamed, "Are you trying to humiliate our girls? Call off your press! (It had been called off late in the first quarter.) You should be ashamed of yourself!" she concluded. After getting over the shock of her tirade, I calmly replied, "Look lady, why don't you talk to your coach so she can teach her players to break our defense?" I figured she isolated her wrath on me because I was the oldest coach on the bench. When she approached me and started her shouting, I thought about pointing to Coach Jeff Jacobson, who was sitting next to me and passing the blame to him. But I vetoed that idea – I couldn't do that to my son-in-law. Oh well! The upset mother seemed mollified as she marched back across the floor, meanwhile not paying attention to the action on the court.

In my last year of coaching in February 2008, our Bluejacket girls finished their regular schedule with a big win over Chisholm on the Bluestreak's court. After the game was over, several of my team members came over and game me our normal congratulatory hugs. I even received a hug from two of the Chisholm girls who I knew very well. About this time a man walked up to me and declared, "I ought to report you to the police. You're a damn pedophile – I saw how you were fondling those girls." Then he briskly walked away and was lost in the crowd leaving the gym. I was stunned by this encounter and for once in my life, actually speechless! This bothered me quite a bit and in the next few days I asked some of the parents of our girls if the hugging bothered them. All of them assured me that it was not a bother and their daughters would be upset if they didn't get a hug from me occasionally. Normally, I don't

Fifty-Five Years on the Bench

initiate the hugs, but I always return them. My girls will always be special to me, but at least one very misguided individual will never understand this.

These past extraordinary events just described, which have dotted my professional career, are unforgettable. Not included are the many little mishaps that occur during practices and games. A practice move during a junior college workout led the way to my first knee surgery. Coach Schmitz and I were conducting drills when I saw a loose ball rolling down the court and entering the drill area. I sprinted after the ball and immediately felt a stabbing pain in my right knee. I couldn't straighten out my leg and upon further examination by an orthopedic surgeon, found I had torn my meniscus lining in the knee. I was in surgery one week later.

On several occasions, as I wandered under baskets where team members were shooting, a stray shot usually found my face instead of the hoop. I've had several pairs of glasses shattered, in addition to suffering cuts on the nose and forehead. You would think I would have learned my lesson, but I guess I was a slow learner.

Take a bath with your clothes on? As a coach, especially if you're on the winning side, you may undergo this experience. In 1972, as an assistant coach for the Hibbing Cardinal football team, we had just defeated Mesabi State Junior College to win the conference championship. When we all got into the locker room, the happy Cardinal gridders took all four coaches and threw us in the showers where we proceeded to get soaked. I had my 8-year old son, Don, with me and, thinking the worst, he broke out in tears, believing the players were hurting me. I had to do some quick explaining to assure him that we were just celebrating.

Another bath I took happened in St. Cloud, Minnesota as our powerhouse 8th grade basketball team won a Pacesetter Tournament championship. Upon completion of the game, the team wanted to go outside (the tourney was in July), for the team picture. Doug and I didn't think anything unusual about the outdoors placement and went out with the team to honor their request. They insisted that the two coaches get in the front row on bended knees and we proceeded to do so. That's when

Richard W. Varichak

we felt the deluge of water as the team emptied all their water bottles on us. Hannah Miesbauer, in her memory paper, did say, "I remember winning a Pacesetter Tourney and pouring water on you and Doug, but we all went mostly for Doug because we didn't want you to get all wet." Then one wonders why we love those girls!

When asked why I remained in coaching for all these years, I give credit to a warm and fulfilling relationship that developed among my players and coaches, especially with Doug. I also looked forward to each day's experience because I knew that there wouldn't be any boring hours. It's no wonder why 55 years passed so quickly.

Chapter 9: Nine Talented Ladies - They Turned the Program Around

There are certain periods of your coaching life when a group of players come along to make your experience such a joy and solidify your decision to be a coach. Doug and I went through this period of time when we inherited a talented group of 7th graders. Doug had just been hired in Hibbing to administer the Mesabi Trail program and I had finished up one year coaching the 8th grade and Varsity girls. I already

Figure 26: Photo by John Peterson
Hibbing High School 7th Grade Basketball Team
2001-02: 27 wins – 3 losses
Front row: Holly Yarosak, Jodi Schmitz
Second row: Mgr. Amanda Incontro, Tammy Simons, Mallory Donahur, Jessica Lubovich
Third row: Coach Doug Schmitz, Nicole Nyberg, Nikki Klinck, Stacy Burdick, Hannah Miesbauer, Lindsay Jacobson, Coach Dick Varichak

Fifty-Five Years on the Bench

had coaching stints with the Washington Elementary girls where I had Vanessa and Shawna, my grand-daughters, playing for me. I approached Doug about helping out and serving as co-coaches of our 7th graders and he agreed. We had 18 girls interested in playing so we decided to divide the squad into a blue team and a white team. Doug and I took the "blue squad," which had the better players, and Brian Karich took the "white squad." Our philosophy with the junior high players was to make sure everyone got in the game. Fortunately, our starters were in the habit of building up big leads early so there was no trouble in playing everyone. Seven of the original "fab nine" played on that blue team. The other two we put on the white team to try and balance the skills for each team.

Figure 27: Game Program photos by Larry Ryan

When we started practices, we noticed that this was a very intelligent group of athletes. We discussed teaching some advanced skills, realizing that these kids could master them. There was unusual quickness with lightening quick Nikki Klinck, Stacy Burdick and Jodi Schmitz. Complementing this speed were sharp-shooting Lindsay Jacobson, Nicole Nyberg, and Kelly Manney. Stevie Pelkey, Amber Brant, and

Richard W. Varichak

Hannah Miesbauer gave us low-post strength and under the basket scoring.

It took our first game against Virginia in their old Roosevelt gym to see just how good this team could be. Although Virginia was much taller than our half-pints, they couldn't keep up with our speed and quickness. We utilized the full-court press and rolled to a 27-1 lead early in the game. Virginia did not get a shot at the basket until there was only 1:27 left in the opening quarter. We scored 93 points and were on our way to many more blowouts.

We thought our kids could handle a full-court zone press, half-court zone press, three-quarter zone press in addition to a 1-2-2 zone defense. Our presses would be utilized after different situations. For instance, the full-court press would go into operation after we scored a basket. The half-court press would go into action after we shot a free throw. The three-quarter press was normally used to slow up the opponent's offense when our lead was being threatened. We always stressed to our team, if you want to rest during a game, do it on offense! Your best work happens on defense and it worked for our club as they scored many points on opponent's mistakes.

This talented group gave us quite a few highlights in the next two years. They raced to a 27-3 record as 7th graders and a 33-7 slate against their 8th grade competition. Only one defeat in two years was administered by Range schools, a 33-31 loss to Chisholm. The other 9 setbacks were at the hands of AAU and All-star teams in St. Cloud, Rochester and Minneapolis.

An 8th grade state championship in St. Cloud during Pacesetter play, highlighted one of our finest performances. A victory over New London-Spicer in semi-final play reflected what superb defense can do to gain the win. New London-Spicer led at half-time 10-8 with 8 of their points scored by their tall, talented center. We then put on a defensive show for the remainder of the game. Hibbing held the Wildcats without a field goal for the entire second half and through three overtimes, which amounted to 22 total minutes of play. Meanwhile, Lindsay Jacobson hit a last second basket to send the game into the third extra session and the

Fifty-Five Years on the Bench

young Jackets hung on to win 18-16. To add to the drama, Stacy Burdick connected for a 2-pointer to send the game into its first overtime. Doug and I were as drained physically as our players who battled for 38 minutes of the toughest defensive action in the tournament.

The 18-16 win over New London-Spicer was a semi-final win following a thrilling 26-25 overtime victory over Kingsland in the tourney opener. Facing us in the state championship game was Worthington and our kids came through in another nail-biter 23-20. The remarkable thing about this championship was it was accomplished without two key players. Our leading scorer from the 7th grade season, Nikki Klinck, had been brought up to the Varsity team. So we lost her 15 points per game. Andrea Paul, our 6-foot pivot, who played with us for most of the season, had to leave the team because her family moved back to the Twin Cities. This seemed to solidify the rest of the players and game performance never fell off.

Our kids also experienced a big come down in one of our Pacesetter Tourneys in Rochester. After blowing away teams on the Range and scoring 70 to 90 points in many of the games, our half-pints found out what it felt like to be on the other side. In a game against an Austin All-Star club, we found other teams could press and score. Hibbing fell behind early as Austin scored easy baskets when we found out we couldn't handle their suffocating press. Half-time found us trailing 29-12 and our dawbers really down. This was a new experience for our kids and they had a hard time believing the score. It didn't get any better the second half and soon the decision was made to play running time. What a down beat! We finally left the floor with a 59-24 loss and I felt the team learned a valuable lesson.

We usually put in a special play to be used only when it's necessary to score or prevent a score. We introduced a special move called "banana." This constituted a full-length court pass from out-of-bounds and the success ratio of this play was very slim. We did use it against Chisholm in one of our barn-burner games in Hibbing. We had the ball out-of-bounds, trailing 28-27, and needed to go the entire 84 feet to our basket. We placed Nicole Nyberg, who had the strongest arm, as the

Richard W. Varichak

throw-in player from out-of-bounds. As the play started, Nyberg wound up, delivered a long pass to Stevie Pelkey breaking towards the basket where she made the catch and drove in for the winning score at the buzzer. So, a play like this is run through several times a week in practice and it may work very seldom, but it's nice to have it in your options.

The "fab nine" also revealed themselves as pranksters when the situation called for some fun and humor. After winning the State Pacesetter crown in St. Cloud, our team picture was set up outside on the parking lot. When the photographer said "cheese," both Doug and I felt a deluge of water as all the players poured their water bottles on us.

When this team became varsity players (I believe they were juniors), they were responsible again for some more tomfoolery. On a road trip to the Twin Cities, we were at our motel after a Friday night loss to Wayzata. The team was a little down in the mouth because the loss snapped our win string at 19 games and knocked us out of the unbeaten ranks. Although disappointed, Doug and I still were proud of our 19-1 record. While waiting for a late pizza meal, both of us were instructed to leave our room and join the team in the motel lobby. We did so and enjoyed the meal with the team, not realizing that some of the team members were absent. When we returned to our room, what a surprise awaited us as we came through the door. The date that day was February 14th – Valentine's Day – and we discovered the room filled with balloons and a message for each of us on our pillows – "We love you Coach!" What a glorious surprise - until we went into the bathroom and found our tub filled with goldfish swimming about. Do you wonder why we love these kids so much?

Our final connection as coaches with these super kids ended with their play in the state basketball tournament in March 2007. Although we lost to a tough DeLasalle team by a 50-37 margin, these nine young ladies came all the way to the top of their athletic and academic lives. I told them as 7th graders that they would lead us into the state tournament as varsity players and every one of them sincerely believed that they could do this. We, as coaches, couldn't be any prouder!

Fifty-Five Years on the Bench

Figure 28: Photo by Sandy Ongaro
Section 7AAA Basketball Champions – 2007
Hibbing – 76 VS Duluth East – 63
After Game Celebration
Coach Schmitz, daughter Jodi. Coach Varichak, grand-daughter Lindsay, father Coach Jacobson. Daughter Ashley, father Coach Helstrom.

    Our nine kids are now high school graduates and all have gone on to college. Three of the nine pursued college athletics competition and all nine are active in their academic endeavors. Nikki Klinck is a junior at Hamline University where she is a vital part of the Piper basketball program.

    Grand-daughter Lindsay Jacobson is in her junior year at the University of Minnesota-Morris, majoring in English and serves as the Libero on the Cougar Volleyball Team. Lindsay also was a two-year letter winner with the Hibbing Cardinal Volleyball and Basketball teams. She served as captain in both sports as well as gaining All-Conference and All-Region honors. She was instrumental in leading the HCC volleyball team to a third place finish in the National Tournament.

    Nicole Nyberg began her college studies at the College of St. Scholastica for one year then transferred to Hibbing Community College where she led the Cardinal basketball team in scoring and 3-point

Richard W. Varichak

leadership. Nicole is now a junior math major at the University of Minnesota – Morris but is not competing athletically.

Jodi Schmitz is following in Doug and Kathy Schmitz's footsteps and is now a junior at the University of Minnesota- Minneapolis. Her two older sisters, Julie and Katie are also University of Minnesota graduates. Julie now working with the U.S. Olympics and Katie, like her parents, is employed in the teaching profession. My request to Jodi to "dunk" for the Gopher basketball team draws a roll of the eyes and a "you bet coach" answer from our diminutive point guard. She is now working as an intern in the Gopher Athletic Department.

Figure 29: Photos by Larry Ryan

Stacy Burdick is following a career in nursing and is finishing her two years of college at Hibbing Community College. Stevie Pelkey started her post high school studies at Hibbing Community College and is now working full-time. I hope she can resume her studies and maybe play some more basketball. Kelly Manney and Amber Brant have matriculated at St. Scholastica and although not connected with athletics, are still top-notch students. Hannah Miesbauer went out west and is now a junior at

Fifty-Five Years on the Bench

North Dakota University in Grand Forks. When Hannah first started playing for us in 7th grade she told us she didn't know what hand to use when attempting a shot at the bucket. Later, she discovered her left hand worked best and throughout the years, developed an accurate southpaw 15-foot shot.

All nine proved to be excellent students in high school, averaging over 3.0 on their GPA scores. This intellect transferred itself to the basketball court where they demonstrated over and over again their top-flight court sense. Although at times they were pranksters and just "little girls," they made our lives an enjoyable and fulfilling experience.

Figure 30: Photo by Larry Ryan
HIBBING HIGH SCHOOL 2007 BLUEJACKETS
Front row: Stevie Pelkey, Lindsay Jacobson, Amber Brant, Kelly Manney, Nicole Nyberg, Nikki Klinck, Jodi Schmitz, Hannah Meisbauer, Stacy Burdick.
Middle row: Kayla Swanson, Ashley Helstrom, Misa Matetich, Courtney Marschalk, Breanna Chamernick, Hillary Bungarden, Bekah Meisbauer, Laicee Grahek, Melissa Weisbrick, Alisha Harris.
Top row: Coach Varichak, Coach Schmitz, Beth Marklowitz, Melissa Nyberg, Kate Lange, Alia Cook, Dashia VanOverbeke, Molly Stenstrom, Chrissy Rask, Coach Helstrom Coach Jacobson.

Chapter 10: My Senior Citizens - They Came to Play

As a coach on the high school level, you take what grades 7-12 can offer in the way of athletics. These are young student athletes who are still developing both physically and mentally. You deal with immaturity, tantrums, indecisions, love lives and all the experiences which face these kids.

This environment changes when assuming coaching positions on the college level. We, at the community college level, usually get the 18 and 19 year old students in their first two years of college matriculation. It is not unusual to have an older student who decides to participate in inter-collegiate athletics. During my tenure as a college coach, I had the opportunity to be involved with several older student athletes and the experience proved truly enjoyable.

One of the most memorable older student athlete who I had the pleasure of coaching was Judy Lipovetz. Judy was 42 years young and had been out of school for quite a few years, raising three children and being a solid partner with husband, Jerry. I was serving as the Women's Tennis Coach and I knew that Judy had been playing tennis quite often at our local athletic club. But I will let Judy talk of her community college tennis experience as she related to me, sports editor Mark Stodghill of our local paper and Howard Singer of the Minneapolis Tribune. The following is the written description she offered to us in 1981.

"LUV and Me"

My first choice for a title was, "Can a Forty-two Year Old Mother of Three be Recruited into the Closed Ranks of College Tennis Competition and Survive?" But there wasn't enough room on the top line.

My tennis days go back about six years ago, when some friends and I discovered that the game didn't have to end with a serve. Fortunately, my family wasn't immune to its siren call either and with the help of the City Indoor Club and our own back yard court, we all played semi-

Fifty-Five Years on the Bench

regularly all year long. Phil Donahue, the T.V. game shows, and yes, even eating, now hold a distant second, third and fourth place in my priorities.

The present state of affairs really began on a rainy, miserable day in November. I gathered all my courage and with my son, already a freshman at the college, leading and pointing directions, I found myself in the Guidance Center. I asked many questions and received answers such as, "Yes we do have all your records from way back when and yes, your English credits do transfer and yes, you should register for winter quarter beginning in two weeks."

Afraid of changing my mind if I thought too much more about it, I quickly registered for my classes. Upon completion of this action, I then felt a surge of elation and exclaimed to no one in particular, "Here I come, academic world."

I had been telling myself for twenty years now that "someday" when the kids are older and I have more time, etc., etc., I would go back to school. Well, "someday" had actually arrived. The very hardest part was finding the Guidance Center and convincing myself that I could once again settle down into a college student's routine.

Back to tennis and a most surprising phone call from Dick Varichak this spring. He is the coach of the Women's Varsity Tennis team and wanted me to play for him. How flattering! How fun! How ridiculous! Thanks, Coach, but no thanks. Fortunately, the Coach must have caught a note in my voice that was yearning to say yes, and he kept calling. In the meantime, between phone calls, that is, I took a survey of those people nearest and dearest to me and whose opinions I most value.

First, the children. Jeffrey, age thirteen, exclaimed, "Wow! You're going to do it aren't you? You can do it. Do it!"

Jerry, age nineteen, is the one, in my mind, who should have been the most upset over this frivolity. I tried to place myself in his shoes and decided that if I were he, I would be horrified to have my mother play collegiate tennis especially at the same school I was attending, being that I was on the Men's team. I was very content to have my mother stay at home and keep the cookie jar full of homemade goodies. Happily, Jerry

Richard W. Varichak

isn't narrow-minded. He keeps telling me he's proud and has adjusted to the Elves' Keebler cookies.

Our eldest child, Jennifer, is a junior at a college in the metropolitan area of the state, so it didn't have such an impact on her and I was fairly certain of her response. She has always encouraged my zanier side and was tickled with the whole idea.

My husband, Jerry, didn't exactly do hand stands at the initial idea, but has now become my best fan, pinning up my press clippings all over the house and sending information to relatives and encouraging me at the matches.

One of my best friends, representing all the women I play tennis with, thought it was super and a chance not to be missed. When I expressed doubt as to what people might think, she replied, "Everyone who plays tennis thinks it's great. Those who don't think we're all crazy anyway so why worry about them?"

All of this positive feedback has given me a sense of confidence like I've never felt before. Like many people, I've spent far too much time worrying about whether people like me or not. Now, I know many people think I'm going through my second childhood. The most wonderful thing I've discovered about myself is that it's okay for them to feel that way as it really doesn't bother me. What a therapeutic attitude! What a stepping stone, at last towards my own maturity. Hopefully, there will be many more stones to follow.

The tennis team had already been in practice for a week when I joined them. I'm sure they were curious and I felt very ill at ease at first. One of the beauties of tennis is that you don't have time to worry about anything but returning the ball. The captain of the team, Nancy Fiori, was the catalyst in my decision to play. She has been a good friend since I met her when she was playing with my daughter on the local high school team. She is so talented and playing doubles with her is a pure joy. Her humor and supportiveness have really been a boost. The team as a whole seems to have accepted me and I feel privileged to have become better acquainted with a few of them, a bonus for sure.

Fifty-Five Years on the Bench

Our coach, Dick Varichak, has to be one of the warmest, sincerest, up-beat persons I've ever met. He has such rapport with all the students. One has the feeling of trying a little harder just to see him smile a little broader.

As I sit here writing this, I have one week of tennis to go and I will be sad when it's over, but the memories will last. Perhaps I will have given my future grandchildren material to write themes about.

Or perhaps it won't end. Wimbledon may recruit me next year and from there I'll go on tour with the Grand Masters Tennis Traveling Antique Show. Wherever it ends, it has been great therapy and fully enriched my life.

Probably one of my favorite elders who came under my guidance was my younger brother, George, or as we know him, "Butch." He was not interested in going to college when he finished high school in 1957. Because of his bout with rheumatic fever and subsequent heart problems, he didn't get a chance to participate in athletics until his junior year in high school. He was finally allowed to play both football and basketball in his last two years of high school and proved to be a good basketball player.

Figure 31: Photo by Orville Olson
Judy Lipovetz

He moved to the west coast with the family and found employment with Boeing Aircraft. My brother, Kenny, was already settled in Seattle and helped both Butch and my dad to obtain employment with Boeing. I was hired by Hibbing Junior College in the spring of 1963 and had to pick up four credits of community health in order to teach that course at Hibbing. I decided to take the credits at the University of

Richard W. Varichak

Washington, plus a CPR course, and moved my family for the summer to Seattle to stay with my parents. My classes were in the morning so I had the rest of the day free. I asked my dad and brother if Boeing hired part-time help, hoping that I could fill in my free time and make a little money in the afternoon. Butch came with me to the Boeing Employment Office and warned me that we probably would have to sit around for days waiting for a work decision. After filling out the necessary forms, we sat down to wait. Surprisingly, ten minutes later I was requested to go to the Professional Services office where I was offered full-time employment. Butch was greatly surprised and didn't say anything on the way home. When we got to my parents' home, he went to his wife and announced, "Pat, pack our bags, we're going to Hibbing and I'm going to go to Hibbing Junior College." He was duly impressed with what a Masters Degree could accomplish in the pursuit of a job and made up his mind to go the college route.

Butch followed up on his academic and athletic objectives and enrolled at Hibbing Junior College on September 4, 1963. At 24 years old, married with one child and one on the way, he became my first senior citizen to play for me in a school setting. In his freshmen year, he joined the basketball team and became a member of one of my finest teams in my coaching profession. Butch stood 5'11" and served as my starting center – can you believe I had the trust in a 24 year old standing smaller than six feet? Actually my tallest starter that year was sophomore Don Stahl at 6'0" but boy could he shoot that basketball. He was complemented on the front line by Bill Skarich, Pete Kinney, and Bob Sinko, all measuring up at 5'10". Butch was the blue collar worker. He was an excellent rebounder who had learned the ins and outs of working the boards in the tough Seattle basketball league. He also could light up the scoreboard by scoring a lot of "garbage" shots around the hoop which were occasionally missed by our perimeter players. His 27 point outburst against Gogebic Junior College proved he deserved a scoring touch.

He was a Physical Education major, so he had me as an instructor for many classes. He always maintained he couldn't address me as Mr. Varichak – it was too awkward for him. When we were by ourselves, he

Fifty-Five Years on the Bench

called me "Sonny," my boyhood nickname. On the court or in class it was always "Coach." Because of his heart condition, I had to monitor his playing time and had a doctor who sat right behind our bench and directed this time element. He became a pretty good student and eventually graduated from HJC. His Associate of Science degree led him to transfer to the University of Washington in Seattle where he received his Bachelors degree two years later.

Figure 32: Photo by Noka Varichak
George "Butch" Varichak – 24 year old former Chisholm Cager was the starting center on the Hibbing Cardinals BB team.

One of Butch's close high school friends, who was our next door neighbor growing up, also ended up as an older athlete in my coaching tenure. Gary Holland opted to enter the military path and enlisted in the U.S. Marine Corps. After his 3-year hitch, he enrolled at Hibbing J.C. and decided he wanted to play some more football. He performed as one of our linebackers for head coach Joe Milinovich and was a cog on the Cardinal defense. Although not exceedingly fast, he was a tough hitter and not afraid of the heavy contact that occurs on the college level.

My first association with Butch and Gary, as a coach, actually came nine years earlier in the summer of 1954. I was on a 30-day leave from the Navy after being transferred from Naval Air Station, Moffet Field, California to a Naval Air Station in Kingsville, Texas. Chisholm Recreation Director, Swede Pergol, asked me to coach the Chisholm Midget Baseball team in the forthcoming annual Range Midget Tournament. Both Butch and Gary were members of the team, Butch the third

Richard W. Varichak

baseman and Gary, a pitcher and outfielder. I accepted the assignment and looked forward to working with the 14-15 year olds, most of whom I knew well. Having played in the tournament myself, 10 years earlier, I knew that this was the biggest playoff series on the Iron Range for 15 year olds. I was also fortunate to play on three championship teams as we dominated the competition in that time period.

We fought our way to the championship game only to lose to a powerhouse Hibbing team led by Nick Maras, who went on to pitch for the Pittsburgh Pirates a few years later. Butch and Gary were integral parts of that team and gave me a feeling of accomplishment and satisfaction in that short 30-day experience.

One of my favorite football players at Hibbing Community College came in at 22 years of age and originally was in the Law Enforcement Program. Mike Olson was a Hibbing high school wrestler and

Figure 33: Photo by Al Higgins - HCC
Mike Olson – 25 year old football star at Hibbing Community College 1983-84.
All-Conference Offensive Guard

although not overly big, was a hard-nose guard and defensive lineman for me. My son, Don, was my quarterback and Mike took it upon himself to be Don's personal guardian on the football field. He would not put up with an opponent roughing up his QB and on several occasions, drew some unnecessary roughness penalties when he felt Don was being mistreated. Mike eventually switched his major field of study to education

Fifty-Five Years on the Bench

and served as co-captain along with Don in their sophomore year. Mike transferred to the University of Wisconsin – Superior where he played on one of the last UW Superior teams before they dropped the sport. He is now the Activities Director at Little Falls High School. He said he left my coaching philosophy with a very important lesson which he carried over in his own coaching life. In Mike's words: "One lesson I will always remember and one I have used many times was the experience we had playing Vermilion Community College. As you remember, we were defeated in our final football game and Vermilion continued to pour it on until the end. I think the final score was like 53-6 or something like that. It made me angry. Two or three years later we were coaching together. I was helping with the offensive line. We had a decent team and we were beating Vermilion by a large score. I wanted to keep running the score up and you quietly said to me, "Mike, those aren't the kids who played against you." You were right! There have been many times I have reminded the coaches I am in charge of the lesson I learned. To always be conscious of the kids who are playing. Do not let personal feelings influence your judgment. I have also tried to always keep the kids first in my decision. A lesson you helped instill in me – Thank you for that!

Mike made coaching fun for me and I knew he would be a success as a coach and a leader in educational circles.

Jim Decker came into our college family as an ex-paratrooper from Austin, Minnesota. A feisty 23-year old, he was the nephew of our Athletic Director, Mario Retica. Jim performed at a point guard position, only 5'8", but tough defensively and could be a scoring threat from the outside. He broke into the starting lineup in his freshman year and helped lead our team to a 12-2 conference record and 14-7 overall. He gave the team some leadership qualities and was a fierce competitor. Jim was somewhat of a cynic and was extremely judgmental. Some of his negative attitudes bothered his teammates to a point where players could not get close to him. Our chemistry on the team in his second year was not the best and I noticed a division in team loyalties. Midway through his sophomore year he broke a team rule which necessitated his removal from the squad. We lost a pretty good player but I did notice the team

Richard W. Varichak

chemistry improved considerably. It was not the best experience in my coaching career.

As I mentioned in Chapter One, in my coaching relationship with older players I found them somewhat more mature, less prone to buckle under pressure, and sometimes it was nice to converse with others closer to my age.

The community college athletic programs are able to provide opportunities to older students who decide to return to school for a variety of reasons. My Hibbing Cardinals had the pleasure (or displeasure) to face a couple of "old timers" who came back to their respective schools and honed their basketball skills. Mark Stodghill, a 6'2" shooting guard and 23-years old, spent four years in the Air Force then enrolled at Inver Hills State Junior College in St. Paul, Minnesota. He was a big force for the St. Paul College five and led the club in scoring in those first two years. Mark took his athletic prowess to Macalester for his final two years and upon graduation became a solid journalist. He accepted a position with the Hibbing Daily Tribune as their sports editor, but it was not the first time that Mark came into my coaching tenure. He helped run my Cardinals out of the gym as a player with Inver Hills in a 73-37 defeat during his freshman year. I had a chance to work closely with him in my position as the Athletic Director and Sports Information Officers at HJC. He now works for the Duluth News Tribune following court and crimes cases.

Tom Otterdahl proved that being an older player could be a benefit to college programs. A graduate of Bloomington High School, Tom went into the work force in the construction field. Finally, at 29 years of age, he decided to go back to school and enrolled at Normandale Community College. In Bloomington, not only did Tom lead Normandale to a pair of successful seasons, he also was a contributor to the St. Thomas University basketball program. He was the oldest player in the MIAC and the only player older than Stodghill (according to Mark). What a great pair of senior citizen athletes!

Back to junior college football and a couple more seniors who chose to wear a Cardinal uniform. Marty Churpurdia was a 28-year old

Fifty-Five Years on the Bench

fullback who decided he wanted to play some more football. Not a speed demon, Marty was more of a bruising type of runner and got the hard-to-get yards. Then we had a definite blue collar football player on the defensive side of the ball in the person of Dennis Grcevich, whose only drawback was his poor eyesight. He was one of the few players who wore glasses on the field. His big moment on the field occurred on a rainy day against Brandon College from Winnipeg, Canada. He picked off an errant Brandon forward pass and rambled 65 yards for a touchdown. Of course, it took him most of the afternoon to run those 65 yards. A speed demon he was not!

One of the most pleasant older students who came my way was an outstanding 23-year old athlete from California. Darron Riley or, "Irish" as we called him, was 6'6" African-American and an outstanding athlete. He came to us to basically play basketball, but also finished two years of football, although he did not play the sport in high school. He was a man among boys on both the football field and basketball court and helped both our teams to successful seasons. He was a wide receiver and punt returner for me on the gridiron and in a home game against Vermilion, scored five touchdowns, 3 on passes and 2 returning punts. He was just as effective in the basketball wars, leading Doug Schmitz's cagers in scoring, rebounding, and blocked shots. Darron went on to a sales profession and has done very well after his college experience.

I enjoyed the situation when a student desired to participate in inter-collegiate sports and it was obvious he or she was not high school vintage. In the cases of Darron Riley and Judy Lipovetz, or my brother, Butch, I wasn't too worried about their ability to perform at our level. Some of the applicants dropped out shortly after the first few days when they realized that their performance level or time constraints preventing them from competing on a college team. It's just fortunate that the community college system can give our senior citizen athletes the opportunity to compete and enjoy inter-school competition.

Chapter 11: The Highs and Lows of Coaching

In the world of the coaching profession, I don't believe one can go through one's tenure without the highs and lows of competition. As a college instructor at Hibbing Community College, I lectured to future coaches in my classes not to get too high or too low in your wins and losses. Unfortunately, I didn't practice what I preached in my early coaching years as I found myself dipping low in disappointment and on cloud nine when the scoreboard was in my favor. The positive factor in my progress as a coach was that I became more consistent in my behavior towards wins and losses and did not get too high or low. Sometimes it became very difficult not to get too emotional, but it probably helped to retain my sanity and kept my love for coaching intact.

I believe my first coaching disappointment happened on the baseball field. Finding ourselves in the championship game of the Chisholm Midget baseball tourney, my young over-achievers were leading an athletic Hibbing team 4-1 going into the 5th inning of the 7-inning contest. My pitcher, Bob Margo, had the heavy hitting Bluejacket nine completely baffled with his soft dipsy-doodle offerings. I could feel the big upset coming and then – catastrophe struck! Margo, attempting to score, slid into home and fractured his ankle. When I changed pitchers, I had to go to Gary Holland, a fastball thrower. Although Gary tried to keep the lead, Hibbing had the fastball hitters and we eventually lost the lead and the game. It was a deep disappointment for me, but I felt disappointed more so for the kids. We had a lot of tears after the game.

With one of my finest teams at the community college, a play-off loss really hit me hard. My 1969 club, featuring All-American Frank Russ, faced Gogebic Junior College in a one game playoff in Hibbing to advance to the Region 13 championship. We had defeated the other two teams (Mesabi and UM – Crookston) along with Gogebic, so I figured we had a good chance to get to the Nationals in Hutchinson, Kansas. Our only problem was I had two of my starters missing, both suffering

Fifty-Five Years on the Bench

from hepatitis. We later found out that drinking from the same water bottles during timeouts was the culprit in spreading the condition. The game went down to the final seconds with the Cardinals holding a one point lead. Gogebic had a chance to score with eight seconds left and took a shot which came off the backboard. The rebound shot was put up and went through the hoop at the buzzer and we were one point losers. Not only was the loss a deep hurt, all team members and cheerleaders had to undergo Gamma Globulin shots to combat the effects of hepatitis and that included me and Tom Anzelc, my assistant. Alas! The loss to Gogebic hurt worse than the needle!

Another low point in my coaching life came over a complete season and occurred after a series of games. The season of 1973-74 with the Men's Cardinal Basketball team proved to be one of the weirdest and disappointing seasons. With top-notch student athletes like sophomores Doug Schmitz, Rick Stark, Bob Eggers, Wade Olson, and Tom Gornick, the season looked very promising. We ended up with a 6 win- 16 loss record and the worst part of the year was losing ten contests in overtime, at the buzzer, or last second shots. This is the team that went into games thinking, "How are we going to lose tonight?" I started to doubt my coaching strength because my thought centered on the fact that I had good players and we were still losing. It had to be some shortcoming on my part! We had talented players who were excellent students, great attitudes, and good chemistry among the team as a whole. I'm still at a loss to find the answers to that year.

Years later, when I was coaching the Hibbing High School Girls' Basketball team with Doug Schmitz, a playoff loss to Hermantown High School proved to be one of my most disappointing coaching experiences. Our ball club, led by talented Anna Matetich, Emma Jaynes, and Nikki Klinck, came into the game with a 26-1 record and holding a win over the Hawks earlier in the season. As expected, the game turned out to be a thriller and the excitement level was sky high. The gym at Denfeld High School was packed and the noise level was ear-splitting. High school basketball at its most entertaining!! The game went down to the final seconds with Hibbing holding a two-point lead. Nikki Klinck stole the

Richard W. Varichak

ball at that point, started to drive down court and was fouled. With all the noise and screaming, our girls thought the game was over and three of our reserves raced onto the floor to hug Nikki. Unfortunately, there were still a couple of seconds left and the Hermantown bench started calling for a technical foul on our team for running onto the court. One official was trying to wave our girls off the floor, but the other official proceeded to assess our team with the technical. Needless to say, both Doug and I were shocked at his decision because we felt the basis of the rule was not violated. But we also felt the game was still in our hands. Nikki had two free throws and all she had to do was make one. She missed both shots while Anna Bjorin, their star guard, knocked down both of her attempts to tie the score and send the game into overtime. The four minutes of extra playing time was just as exciting as the preceding 36 and the game was decided on a last second shot by Hermantown to win the game 89-88. My feeling, at the buzzer ending the game, was one of numbness – I just couldn't believe how it ended.

This was a potential state tournament team and we probably would have been very competitive in the state playoffs. We did have a chance to win at the end but we still felt the turning point of the game was the terrible decision made by the official. Most of all, we felt extremely sorry for the kids – they didn't deserve the outcome.

One year later, the deep disappointment changed to high expectations, once again, tied to the girls' cage program. Our "fab nine" were now seniors and behind the leadership and talents of Nikki Klinck, Nicole Nyberg, Lindsay Jacobson, Jodi Schmitz, and Amber Brant, the Bluejackets once again went into the Section 7 championship game with a 23-4 record. Our foe that night was a tough Duluth East five who had given us one of our four losses during the season. Playing in front of our hometown fans in the Hibbing Memorial Building, our fired-up team raced to a commanding 19-point lead at half-time and went on to claim the Section crown, and a trip to the State Tournament. Contrary to my feeling of numbness a year earlier in our loss to Hermantown, I felt myself on cloud nine with this victory. The girls reminded me (between hugs), that I had predicted they would take us to the State Playoffs when

Fifty-Five Years on the Bench

they were competing on the seventh grade level. I truly saw their potential at that time and never failed to think otherwise.

We lost our opening game in the State to a superior DeLaSalle team but, all in all, the season was a success and the year was fun and fulfilling from a coaching standpoint.

It's very easy to be congenial and personable on the tail end of a win and/or a championship, but the true test of a professional is how one reacts when adversity sets in. Do you snap at your spouse or kick the dog after a bitter loss? Or can you come home, kiss your spouse and start planning for your next game? Early in my coaching career, I did get moody after a setback and I would let it bother me for a while. As I gained experience, I found facing adversity and bemoaning the fact was a waste of time and thus led me on the path to be a more patient and understanding coach.

I had some low moments in coaching, of which I'm not too proud that reflected some lack of emotional maturity on my part. I mentioned an incident in Chapter Eight when I threw my shoe into the stands after an incident involving two of my players during the game. Frankly, I don't remember the incident, but it was described by Greg Crnkovich, a dedicated and loyal player. Greg would not bend the truth in my estimation and, I do give him credit for truthfulness. I still have a hard time believing I would be so infantile.

Another example of my loss of emotional control happened after a home community college men's' basketball game. I had a small, scrappy, hustling team, led by versatile Greg Staniger, and we were entertaining a very talented Fergus Falls five. Knowing we couldn't match them on the boards, I decided to throw a half-court press to start the game. The move worked to perfection as we raced to a 24-0 lead and it looked like an easy win. But as the game progressed, Fergus settled down, started utilizing their size and slowly started to catch up. We helped them in their efforts as physical and mental errors provided by our sloppy play finally led to an eleven point defeat. When I entered the locker room, thoroughly disgusted with our play, I took my wrath out on a poor waste paper basket that was situated near the door. I attempted to kick the basket sky

Richard W. Varichak

high, but my foot became lodged inside the receptacle. I unsuccessfully tried to dislodge the basket but only succeeded in doing a one-legged dance from one end of the locker room to the other side. This "dance" was the signal for all the team members to burst out in uncontrollable laughter which made me all the more upset. After some time, I did get the basket off my foot (it was damaged by this time) but left the locker room without talking to the team. I figured there was nothing more that my team would find enlightening.

I did get ejected from a game once in my career. It occurred in a conference contest with Gogebic at Ironwood, Michigan. The game evolved into a physical push and shove type of contest which got away from the two elderly officials who should have been retired. Both coaches had complained throughout the game and I had earned a stern warning from one of the dinosaurs earlier in the second half. The incident which led to my dismissal came on a foul by our John Hughes as he attempted a steal. The referee whistled him for the foul and turned to the scoring table to report the violation. John was still holding the ball and I told him, "John, give the ref the ball." John tossed the ball to the official just as he turned around to face the court. The ball accidentally hit him in the face and enraged, he grabbed John's jersey and pushed him toward the sideline and ejected him from the game. I immediately became upset and raced onto the floor, picking up the ref by his shirt collar and told him, "Don't you ever touch one of my players!" The official responded, "Coach, you're out of here, too" and pointed me towards the gym door. There were only two minutes left in the game and we were down by eleven, so I told my team, "Let's go – we're all going to leave." I led the club off the court and we were subjected to hoots and hollers from the Gogebic crowd. Our team manager, Frank Bigelow, was hassled by some of the students and he responded by swinging the bag of basketballs he was carrying, striking some of the jerks. They quickly scattered and got out of Frank's way. When we got in the bus for our trip home, our bus driver confessed he punched a heckler who said something uncomplimentary to him before we got there. We also had a police escort out of Ironwood to the Wisconsin border. The next morning,

Fifty-Five Years on the Bench

Ovie Nordvall, our Dean of the College, told me Hibbing Junior College had been penalized for taking the team off the floor and forfeiting the game. We were assessed a $50.00 fine for my action and I told Ovie I would pay it. He declined the offer and stated the college would take care of the problem. I did get good-natured ribbing from my colleagues and parents for some time.

I received only six technical fouls in my 55 years roaming the sidelines, but got two in one game. We were in Thief River Falls battling a tough Northland Community College squad. We were once again stuck with two officials who should have retired from the game long before. They were slow a foot and got caught out of position numerous times. We were tagged for 29 fouls and Northland 27. Between the two teams there were an unbelievable 77 free throws. Northland converted 40 and Hibbing successfully sank 21 free throws, so both clubs were at the gift line for most of the afternoon. My problem came with free throws as our team was called for six free throw violations (being in the lane too soon), and on the last call, Fred Zbacnik, our leading scorer that day, took the ball and bounced it vehemently off the floor. While the ball was high in the air, the ref slapped Fred with a technical foul. I stepped out on the floor and questioned him about the call and he responded, "Your player bounced the ball off the floor a little too hard in my estimation." My reply was a quick retort, "He should have bounced the ball off your head." Of course, I received an expected "T" but it sure felt good at that time. We lost the game 119-95 and took about four hours to play.

Looking back at my 55 years in the coaching profession, I can honestly say the total experience was a highly positive and exciting one. It was a "job" that I looked forward to each day and enjoyed the various and rewarding highlights of the day.

Chapter 12: You Have to be an Amateur Psychologist to Coach

I slowly began to realize during my coaching experience that I was to wear a variety of hats in my relationship with my players, managers, assistant coaches, and administrators. I found myself in the roles of mentor, father, grandfather, counselor, disciplinarian, and of course, coach. But in dealing with a large variety of personalities, egos, temperaments, and behaviors, I found out that I also became an amateur psychologist. The many athletes I came in contact with ranged in age from 12 years old to the early forties, and both genders were involved.

One of the organizational factors in directing a program was to set up basic team rules and regulations. Some rules were mandated by the sports organizations (Minnesota State High School League, National Junior College Athletic Association, etc.) that governed our competition. But most rules concerning team involvement were authored by the local coaches. Believe me, these rules were varied. Some were strict, some loose, some covered the team as a whole, and some dictated individuals case by case. This is where coaching psychology entered the picture.

One of my biggest obstacles as a coach was to convince people that my decisions were not to benefit the members of my family who came under my coaching umbrella. Unfortunately, many uninformed fans and parents felt that I played a big part in the important roles of competition on their respective athletic teams. I try very hard not to display any favoritism or nepotism in my dealing with family athletes. But part of my so called "psychology" has dealt with them.

In June of 1954, between Navy duty stations, I coached the Chisholm Midget baseball team to a second place finish in the Annual Range Midget Baseball Tournament. My brother, "Butch" was my third baseman and one of the top players on the squad. In our semi-final win, he experienced one of his bad days, both in the field and at the plate. He then mentioned to me that I should replace him at third because he felt he was not good enough to continue as a starter. He shocked me with his request but I knew I would not replace him. My comment to him was,

Fifty-Five Years on the Bench

"Butch, you are my third baseman and you will be my third baseman throughout the tournament." He broke out in the biggest grin I've ever seen and gave me a big hug. The next day against Hibbing in the championship game, he was our biggest offensive weapon and was flawless in the field. We didn't win but he was the best player on the field! Lesson for me as the coach – be loyal to your players no matter how down they feel.

This same brother nine years later, while putting on a Hibbing Junior College basketball shirt, commented, "A lot of people will feel the only reason I'm starting is because you're the coach." I had previously announced my starting lineup for our opener against Gogebic Junior College and he was my starting center. We actually put three forwards and two guards as starters. I didn't feel comfortable listing my starting center at 5'11". My answer to his comment was, "Butch, I put the five best players on the floor as my starters. I consider you one of the five best at this time. The fact that you are my brother has no effect on my decision. You just go out and justify my coaching evaluation." His performance that year proved me right and I know it put him on a higher plane than when he started the program. Lesson number two – use your evaluation expertise to the best of your ability and know it is best for the team.

In my first year at Evant High School in Texas, I had the monumental task in moving an All-District guard (we played with 6 players) for the past three years to a forward in her senior year. The three guards played only on the defensive and couldn't cross the center line. The forwards did all the shooting and scoring and played only their side of the court. She didn't want to move from her comfort level and pleaded with me to keep her at the guard position. I tried to persuade her that she had all the tools to be a high scoring player. She was lightening quick, had a beautiful shot and could rebound. When all my arguments seemed to no avail, I told her to play me one-on-one. I was only 29 years old and in pretty good shape and she knew I could shoot and handle the ball. I told her if I could easily beat her, I would leave her at guard. I also knew as competitive as she was, she would play her hardest.

Richard W. Varichak

We both played hard and she bested me 20-16. She out-quicked me on occasion and beat me to the hoop for some easy layups. Actually, I could have blocked several of those shots but felt her scoring was more important than my blocks. After the game, I reminded her that she defeated a good male college basketball player and just think what she could do against high school girls' competition. With a grin the size of the Colorado River, she told me, "Coach, I think I'm ready to play forward for you." This was punctuated by a high leap in the air and a scream of enjoyment. When my assistant coach, Don Barkley, found out about the switch, he asked me, "How in the hell did you convince her to change?" I gave him a wink and replied, "She dumped me, fair and square – just think what she can do in our upcoming schedule." I don't think Don took me seriously. Carolyn Arnold did everything expected of her, averaging over 25 points a game and became one of the outstanding girl basketball players in the state of Texas. It didn't bother me one bit that a young girl cleaned my clock. At least it paved the way to move her to a forward!

Once again, I was faced with a rule decision in our opening State Junior College game in 1971 with a talented, but troubled freshman athlete named Tom Ronchetti. Tom was a top-notch athlete from Hibbing who just lost his mother in his senior year of high school He was having a difficult time at home and the passing of his mother really affected him. He was hard to reach at first but became a definite starter on our basketball team. My decision evolved as we prepared to open our season on a Thursday night at home. For some reason beyond my control, the game was changed to Saturday evening. When I announced the change to the team, Tom approached me and explained a problem. He had purchased expensive tickets for a concert to be held in Minneapolis on Saturday and was really looking forward to the performance of a very popular music group. Well, my dilemma – a starting guard wants to attend another activity and be lost to his team for one game. I told him I would get back to him in a couple of hours as I wanted to figure something out which would be fair to him and the team.

Fifty-Five Years on the Bench

When I'd had some time to think it through, I explained to Tom that he could attend the concert as it was not his fault that the game night had been changed. I also explained to him the he would have to play with the second unit and work his way back to a starting position. He was surprised at the decision, but readily accepted his demotion. We won the game without him, he served one week on the second unit and then became a starter again the following week. His whole demeanor changed from then on as I noticed his positive acceptance of coaching decisions. Tom continued to be one of our valuable players, both in football and basketball. Now, in his adult years, he has exhibited positive performances as a coach and basketball official. Another lesson learned – take action which benefits both player and team.

A couple of years ago we had several senior girl basketball players who did not see much action during game time. One of these players was Courtney Marschalk, a delightful, energetic, hard-working, young lady who sometimes was disappointed with her playing time. Actually, one of her negative experiences happened because she was on the floor and getting some playing time. We were winning big in a Christmas tourney game and she was playing with several of the younger players in 9th and 8th grade. After the game was over, Courtney and her mother caught me in the hall and Courtney was in tears. She approached me, sobbing and gave me a very wet hug. She was extremely upset from being on the floor with the youngest players we had. She felt humiliated by the experience. She told me she was thinking of quitting. This bothered me. She was the type of student athlete who we need on our teams.

After she settled down I felt a discussion should be held and I wanted especially to keep her from quitting. First of all, I told her playing time was divided up on the more experienced players who had been in the program the longest and had the best skills. I explained to her that she had a late start as a basketball player and lacked some basic skills which slimmed down her playing time. I then proceeded to point out the positive influence that she projected on the team. She was always a sideline cheerleader from the bench. She was coachable; her practice habits were solid and she had to be a quick learner. Her only problem

Richard W. Varichak

was she was behind teammates who were more experienced and had more advanced skills. I told Courtney, "You are a positive influence on this team and I want you to keep playing with us." My emphasis in my statement was, "I want you to keep playing with us." I felt better when Courtney decided to stay on the team and although she didn't get any additional playing time, she did get on the floor with veteran players. I was proud of you, Courtney.

When Doug Schmitz and I started coaching together we decided on a very important rule that we maintained throughout our 20 years with the Hibbing Cardinals, Nashwauk-Keewatin Spartans, and the Hibbing Bluejackets. The two of us have been successful as coaching colleagues, having winning teams wherever we coached. I feel our success not only is based on experience and knowledge of the game, but how we handle our players. Doug is a "type A" personality, one who is quick to anger, demands perfection and gets upset with mental mistakes. He can be harsh in his exchange with players but never means it in a personal nature. He is an excellent bench coach – you won't outcoach him during a game. He is highly organized and prepares his team to a high degree. I am more of a laid-back coach, seldom raising my voice. I reflect the "grandfather" personality but when upset, will raise my decibel level. Just ask my grand-daughter Lindsay. When she heard me beller, "Lindsay Mae!" she knew she had dropped the ball somewhere. But our two personalities have worked quite well in the guidance of our teams and out of this the one important rule was born. When a player is removed from the game, she or he must come out and sit next to me. Normally Doug and I have another assistant sitting between us so the player exiting the game is a couple of coaches away from Doug. He may be upset or concentrating on the play on the floor. So he doesn't get to speak to the player coming out. When the player sits next to me, I explain why they came out, unless it's just to make a position change or the player is in foul trouble. We may take a player out for reasons such as giving them a breather, settling them down if they are committing multiple violations, giving them pertinent instructions on how to play defense or offense or just to soothe their feelings after being chewed out

Fifty-Five Years on the Bench

by Doug. In no way do I countermand Doug's actions or decisions, but I do try and get the player back on the level of game competition. Doug jokingly refers to our actions as "good cop-bad cop" but I don't ever feel that we reflect that behavior. We don't want our players coming out of games, heading for the end of the bench to pout and wonder why they had to come out. The rule has worked for us throughout our coaching tenure and probably has deflected upsetting situations for both coaches and players.

In reading the many letters which I have received to help make this book speak, a certain passage continues to appear. The phrase, "You always seem to care for me, not only as an athlete, but as a person." This statement means more to me than any reference to wins and losses and an evaluation as a coach. Another lesson learned – basic respect and love can go a long way in coaching success. Now I can hand in my "amateur psychologist" license.

Chapter 13: The Players Who Made My Job an Adventure

During my 55 years in the coaching field, I had the occasion to be involved with individuals who made my job exciting and different. These young athletes, through their actions sometimes made me angry, many times gave me a good laugh, occasionally would put me a "rubber room" (driving me crazy), and finally helped me to enjoy the fruits of coaching.

Our coaching staff, throughout the years, had nominated certain players for our "head case" team. We didn't have many candidates for this team but the ones who earned their way on the club certainly deserved the honor. In my estimation, the top player for this group was Bill Skarich, a 5'10 athlete from Nashwauk-Keewatin who played basketball for me in his sophomore year at Hibbing Junior College in 1963-64. I only had him for one year, but I think I would be a definite addition to the rubber room if I had him for two seasons. Incidentally, Skarich fills the bill in all four categories which I mentioned above. Believe me, he was one of the most memorable and enjoyable student athletes in my coaching tenure.

Bill is now 65 years old, a successful retired educator and coach living in Kelly Lake, a few miles out of Hibbing. Noka and I are very happy to have periodic luncheons with Bill and his beautiful wife, Frances. But back to the captain of our "head case" team. Bill reflects a quiet, withdrawn personality who doesn't care for post-season celebrations, dinners and award presentations. I had a heck of a time, getting him to come to our basketball banquet at the end of the year, but thankfully he did appear. He is an extremely gifted individual, tops in academics, a top-notch athlete and a talented musician. He led the junior college football team to a couple of championships from his quarterback position where he excelled, both as a runner and passer. His athleticism also transferred to the track teams where he garnered meet points, both in

Fifty-Five Years on the Bench

high school and college. He performed with a local band, being versatile on both the drums and the keyboard.

Early in our basketball workouts he changed the rules of playing "horse", the game where a player has to match a successful shot of the player before him. Missed shots award the letter "H" through "E" (spelling horse) and eliminate the player from the game. We had some prolific shooters on the team with Skarich, including Pete Kinney, Don Stahl, and Bob Sinko. Bill set the rule that a successful shot must pass through the hoop without touching iron- notably a swisher. I thought, "What arrogance!" But as I watched their horse contests (usually held after practice), I saw most of their successful baskets did swish- I guess that's why we averaged 94 points a game (without the 3-point line), but Bill was not through making my coaching life an adventure in excitement. Although Bill was immaculate in his appearance, his basketball game uniforms did not receive the same cleaning treatment. We noticed after going to our next scheduled contest, when dressing before warm-ups, the uniform he pulled out of his bag was unusually all crumpled up and didn't smell very good. When I accosted him about his dirty, smelly uniform his reply was logical (for Skarich's logic), "Coach, nobody on the other team wants to get near me. I get loose most of the time." I could just shake my head and continually remind him to wash that darn uniform.

Figure 34: Photo by Arnie Maki - HJC
Bill Skarich - Team Captain
All-Conference 1962-64
All-Region 13 1962-64

Richard W. Varichak

Speaking of uniforms, Bill had discovered on a trip to Fergus Falls that he had left his game uniform at home. After counting to ten, I contacted the Fergus coach, Wayne Barham and asked him if he had any spare gear in red, our traveling uniform. Wayne said he only had gold and blue, so we settled for a blue Fergus travel uniform. So there we were four Cardinals in red and Bill in blue. The game went into overtime and Skarich paced us to a 92-90 win. He scorched Fergus with 38 points and played great defense, holding their leading scorer to 8 points. As we prepared to leave, Bill asked coach Barham if he could have the uniform he wore since he had such a great game and felt it would bring him luck in the future. My greatest fear now was he was going to ask me if he could wear this uniform in future games. Wayne solved my problem by refusing Bill's request as I gave a sigh of relief.

We had a key game in Ely against Ely Junior College who were always tough in their home gym. As usual, Bill gave me some anxious moments even before we left Hibbing. He failed to show up at departure time, so we left without him. Fortunately he took his own car and met us at the gym in time for the game. When we dressed, there he was with that crumpled up uniform and his comment, "I forgot to wash it." Seated behind our bench was a long-time Ely sports fan. He started to give Bill some fan razzing, hoping to get his goat and maybe take him off his game. It certainly did not bother our sharpshooter as he drilled home 32 points in our conference win. The Skarich maneuver however, was to race by our bench, point to the fan and hold up two fingers to indicate his successful two points. My only comment to Bill, during a timeout, was, "make sure you hold up *two* fingers all the time." The silence from the fan behind our bench was "deafening"! Skarich strikes again!!

Dave Homoky from Merriville, Indiana was recruited by my replacement at HSJC in 1969 when I left to go to Wyoming University to work on an advanced degree. When I returned from Wyoming a year later, I gratefully inherited Dave for his second year of competition. Dave was a 6'3" jumping jack who had all kinds of offensive moves, but also there wasn't a shot invented that he wouldn't attempt- he tried them all. He had a history of carrying his teammates on his broad shoulders, both

Fifty-Five Years on the Bench

in high school and his two years at Hibbing State J.C. Dave proved to be a friendly, happy-go-lucky individual with loads of talent. His one big fault at first was his lack of attention to coaching suggestions. For a big kid, he had unusual quickness and one of his patented moves was to pick up a defensive rebound and race pell-mell down court for a layup which sometimes went in and sometimes went all over the gym. He was a good shot blocker but occasionally celebrated loudly after each block, giving his opponents a desire to detest him and our team. Repeated efforts to have him perform more team play fell on deaf ears, with numerous apologies from him for his sloppy play and haphazard floor behaviors. We were not very talented that year and he was easily the best player we had and one of the top performers in the conference.

In a road game at Golden Valley Junior College, I finally reached the end of my patience. After he made a number of his mad rushes down court, causing us to lose a hard-earned lead in the first half, I took him out of the game and told him to go sit down on the end of our bench. I kept him out of the game until late in the second half and, although we lost the game, the team performed much better as a unit. His benching seemed to change his approach to the game and we saw a different Homoky in our last few games. He finished his two-year career with a bang in our final contest of the year against UM-Crookston at home. With his parents in attendance, Dave pumped in 42 points to lead us to an 88-84 win. Not only did he move the scoreboard, but he controlled both backboards and played

Figure 35: Photo by Al Higgins - HSJC
Dave Homoky (Merrillville, Indiana)
Hibbing State Junior College 1969-71
All-State 1970-71

stellar defense. Unfortunately we didn't qualify for post-season play so our season was over and the Homoky era came to an end. The great satisfaction which made the whole year worthwhile was a comment from Dave's dad after the Crookston game. He approached me in the locker room and said, "You are the only coach who was able to control David and this has made him a much better player. I believe you have prepared him properly to go on and play four-year college ball." Dave did go on to play at a four-year school and received his Bachelors Degree while playing good, controlled basketball. Although he drove me crazy at times, it was hard to stay upset with him. With his "aw shucks" demeanor, he quickly made you forget his basketball transgressions and he absolutely did not realize that many of his actions and mannerisms brought on numerous bouts of laughter.

We were fortunate to get Ed Tekautz, a 6'5" sharp-shooter from the Chisholm Bluestreaks. Ed was quiet and tended to be somewhat of a loner, although he got along with most of his teammates. He did have a personality conflict with our other center, Greg Crnkovich from Hibbing, and it was apparent that they did not like each other. Knowing male athletic behavior, I thought they would put their differences aside once they got on the basketball floor. But they crossed me up with an incident that came in a game against Northland J.C. in Thief River Falls. I alluded to this situation in a previous chapter.

During the game, after we captured a rebound, Greg and Ed started pushing each other around. I guess Greg had taken offense when Ed had shoved him and said something uncomplimentary. We had to stop the action and I had to escort both players off the floor and tell them to take seats at the end of the bench. In taking this action, I was pulling my two top scorers out of the lineup, and angrily threw my shoe into the stands when Ed complained that he shouldn't come out of the game. I didn't start either player in our next game and without their scoring touch we trailed miserably at half-time. Both players came to me as we returned to the floor and begged to come back in, so I figured they learned their lesson. With both back in the lineup we did make a game of it, but still we lost by two.

Fifty-Five Years on the Bench

Tekautz always came to play hard, was a good scorer and rebounder. Ed did promise me that his differences with other players would be with an opposing player and not a teammate. This comment kept me on the edge of my seat because I didn't know when he would decide to undertake a difference of opinion with an opposing player. His shy smile told me he probably was pulling my chain and really never thought about doing anything nerve-wracking during a game. Although he kept me on my toes with his unpredictable behavior, I thoroughly enjoyed the time he gave me as a college basketball player. Never a dull moment when he was around!

Tom Anzelc came over to HJC from Nashwauk-Keewatin in 1965 as an all-district high school basketball star. Standing at 6'1" with excellent jumping ability, Tom was one of the best shooters to play for me. The only trouble was Tom only

Figure 36: Photo by Arnie Maki - HJC
Ed Tekautz – 1966-67

shot from the corners, the worst spot in the gym, and never followed his attempts because he thought all his shots were good. Although he had good quickness, he thought playing defense was a waste of motion, so when he was on the floor, we were usually playing 4 against 5 on defense. In his first year with us, I usually sought out the weakest offensive player in our opponent's lineup and gave Tom the job of keeping him company. Sometimes it worked and sometimes the strategy backfired.

Tom and I had some heated discussions, especially when I had to take him out of the game because (1) his shot selection was terrible, (2) he didn't rebound, and (3) he was a sieve on defense. He always played hard but he was an individualist and at times it did hurt our game plan. The great transformation for Tom and his development as a player came

Richard W. Varichak

against Virginia J.C., a key conference game in our Lincoln gym. The game was close in the first half, and as usual, Tom was playing his half-spirited game. I finally replaced him and escorted him to the end of the bench. He stomped over to his seat, threw his jacket on the floor and pouted. We played the rest of the first half, all of the second half, and two overtime periods without his services, and won a cliff-hanger. After the game the players deposited their uniforms in a laundry basket to be laundered for the next game. Tom came over to the bin, threw his uniform in, and said to me in an icy tone, "Coach, I never want this to happen to me again." He then stalked off to the locker room. When I went home that evening, I told my wife, "I think we lost one of our top players tonight." I explained to her the details of our confrontation and she agreed that I did the right thing.

On Monday I was pleasantly surprised when Tom showed up, put on his practice gear and went full speed in the workouts. He didn't speak to me for one whole week (he was punishing me!) but I noticed a change of speed and intensity in his practice habits. In our next game he took only half of his normal attempts, shot from different areas on the court and converted three offensive rebounds for scores. But the big difference was his aggressive, tough defensive play.

Needless to say, Tom became one of our most versatile players in his sophomore year; I would assign him on defense to our opponent's best scorer. He became a well-rounded basketball player and later on, a successful history teacher and basketball coach. He's carried these aggressive traits into a successful political life where he has proved to be a tough-nosed legislator. When Tom graduated from St. Thomas University, he applied for a teaching position in Hibbing's Lincoln School. I received a call from Bernie Janesky, the principal at Lincoln, and he asked me to tell him about Mr. Anzelc. It took me only five minutes to tell Bernie to hire that young man and don't let him get away. Tom was immediately hired as a social studies instructor and basketball coach. I was happy and proud to recommend Tom for the job and a chance to repay him for all the joy and wonderful experiences he provided me as his coach.

Fifty-Five Years on the Bench

Going back to Evant High School in Texas during my first year in public school teaching and coaching, I remember two of my athletes who operated on different levels of competition. Both were seniors and both were football linemen. Clynton Smith measured in at 6'3" and 250 pounds, while Eldon Perkins stood 5'8" and 145 pounds. Clynton was an offensive and defensive tackle while "Perk" was my offensive center and doubled as a defensive lineman. Clynton possessed athletic talents and could be over-powering on the football field. He was my power forward on the basketball team and was a bull under the hoop. The trouble I had with the big stud- I didn't know which Clynton was going to show up. At times he would frustrate me with his lackadaisical approach to the game and then turn around and show me just how good he was. My frustration with him also came in the classroom. I met with my seniors each morning at 8:00 a.m. for History and Economic classes. The seniors were very good students as a whole. My only problem was trying to keep Clynton awake during that first hour. I never saw anyone who fell asleep as quick as did my big tackle. It hurt my ego somewhat that someone would fall asleep in my class! But Clynton assured me that his nocturnal episodes were not caused by my instructional methods. He actually admitted that my class was his favorite hour- I often wondered if he was learning something or if he was getting a well-deserved sleep!

I had to find a spot for Eldon because his enthusiasm and dedication was so intense. He weighed in at 145 pounds, soaking wet, and I didn't know where to play him at first. When I held a contest to find a long snapper on punts, Eldon won in a breeze, so I informed him that he was my starting center. I never realized how tough he actually was until we started our game schedule. He was a hard hitter, who took on any opponent who was so unlucky as to be in his sights. He also took his share of punishment as bigger and faster players knocked him around, but I didn't hear one word of complaint or a request to come out of games for rest and recovery when he got his bell rung. Eldon still lives in Evant and organizes cooking tournaments. He even sends me the local Evant newspaper (Evant Star), where he usually has his picture and cooking successes in print. Well done, Eldon! You and Clynton have

Richard W. Varichak

molded my coaching life in different ways, but both have made my professional life a positive and fulfilling experience.

These young student athletes who I bring up as memorable personnel are just a handful of players dotting my coaching calendar. There were others who did not let me get bored and deserved membership in our club, but I will have to emphasize that membership has always been of a positive nature. All of these athletes still hold special spots in my professional and personal life. Players worthy of mention include:

Marcia Buster, Evant High School basketball 1960-62" – exciting player who always kept me on the edge of my seat because I never knew what she was going to do next.

Kathy Cook, Darrouzett High School basketball, 1962-63 – her temper sometimes got her in trouble which made decisions for me, although she was very coachable.

Greg Staniger, Hibbing State Junior College basketball, 1974-76 – one of the best leaders I ever had. Half speed practice player but usually the best player on the floor during games.

Craig Kelly, Hibbing State Junior College basketball – 1979 – never knew which Kelly would show up. Teammates complained about his lack of showers. Could be effective on the basketball floor.

Bob Janezich, Hibbing State Junior College basketball – 1979 – one of my favorites. Although physically handicapped with only one good hand, was very effective on the basketball floor.

Becky Koslowski, Hibbing Community College basketball – 1992 – had trouble keeping her in the game because of fouls. Went 100% all the time – sometimes too hard causing injuries. Died young as the result of an auto accident. Really miss her.!

I guess the key to absorbing the ins and outs of players' behaviors and actions over the years is to put a positive spin on each situation. This may take considerable effort on the coach's part, but it may keep the coach out of the "rubber room."

Chapter 14: Assistant Coaches - A Blessing on the Side

Assistant coaches come in all sizes, intellects, loyalty, and become a key to the head coach's success. I did not experience the comfort of having a true assistant bench coach until I took the head spot at Hibbing Junior College basketball. When I led the Chisholm Midget baseball team in 1954, I did enjoy the company of two assistants. High school classmates and football teammates, Eddie Erickson and Rudy Tomsich offered to help me out for that month. I was home on a 30-day leave from the Navy while Eddie and Rudy had just completed their military obligations and were now civilians. Eddie had some baseball background but Rudy had no idea what baseball was about. In essence, they were cheerleaders, but did help in the few drills we held during practices. When it came to all coaching moves during the game, I was on my own, which didn't bother me. I felt I knew what had to be done and then would carry through.

During my tenure as head basketball coach with the Hibbing Cardinals, I had the pleasure of working with a variety of assistants. I also had some fine assistants as head football coach for the college. My basketball assistants came in different temperaments. They were knowledgeable in basketball procedures, some were quiet and didn't say much, others were vocal and didn't mind voicing their opinion. This latter group included Doug Schmitz, Tom Anzelc and Tammy Sweeney, who used to be my daughter-in-law. Tammy was a third grade teacher at Washington Elementary when I approached her about helping me out with the Hibbing Cardinals women's team. Actually, I was supposed to be the assistant to Dale Hefron who was also serving as the head football coach. Only Hefron failed to show up after the football season and Orville Olson, our Provost, asked me to take the post. I already had a full teaching load so I asked Tammy to assist me. She would get the coaching salary since I couldn't accept the pay. We had all freshmen players and ended up with a 5-15 record, but the girls assured me that they really enjoyed the season. Another lesson learned – the game can still be fun regardless of your win-loss slate. Tammy was very valuable in her role as an assistant and was not afraid to speak up when she had something to contribute. One of her strengths proved to be as a valuable liaison between the players and coaching staff. She was a good listener and helped the girls understand our actions and strategies. She also helped with substituting when I was caught up in the game and would take it upon herself to make a change. I tried to convince her to go into coaching, but she did not want to commit the time and wanted to watch her daughters playing volleyball and basketball. She would have made an excellent coach.

Figure 37: Photo by Al Higgins - Hibbing State Junior College
Tom Anzelc (standing) – Assistant Coach

Another valuable assistant was Tom Anzelc who had just finished college and was teaching at the middle school in Hibbing. Tom was a take charge individual who not only followed my practice schedule to a

Richard W. Varichak

"T," he would volunteer suggestions of his own. He was loud in his instructions and was quick to correct if a player went half-speed in any drill or activity. During ball games he was free with advice which was usually sound and helpful to the team's progress. Because of his strict temperament, some of the players were not overly fond of him, but they all respected him. I was sorry to lose him when he took a coaching position at the high school.

Doug Schmitz as previously noted was like Anzelc, a "type A" personality who could get excited quickly during a game. He easily was the most knowledgeable of all my assistants and I knew he would make a good head coach some day. He recommended drills that he would like to see in our practice sessions and we did utilize many of them. He was a perfectionist and truly believed that repetition on a daily schedule was the answer to improve skills – and – he's right! Doug was not bashful in addressing game officials' mistakes and would let them know what they missed. He was careful, though, not to go too far and receive a technical foul. Doug then took over the head basketball job at the tender age of 24, not much older than his players. He went on to spend 20 years at HCC, 3 years at Nashwauk-Keewatin High School and finished up (for awhile) with 8 years directing the Hibbing Bluejacket girls' basketball program.

Figure 38: Photo by Dick Varichak
Doug Schmitz – Assistant Basketball and Assistant Football Coach

Fifty-Five Years on the Bench

Doug didn't stay inactive very long. Jeff Buffetta, head coach at Mt Iron-Buhl with the girls' basketball program, hired Doug as an assistant where he is now actively coaching.

My other assistants were a little more reserved in their duties and none has gone on to do more coaching. Cal Sabatini, a former Bluejacket great and Minnesota Gopher star, was serving as Sports Editor for the Hibbing Daily Tribune when I persuaded him to come out and do some coaching. Cal usually showed up right from work and worked the practice in his street clothes. He rarely commented during the workouts and didn't say much at our games. The one big advantage of having Cal on the staff was our sports coverage was always prompt and accurate. There were times that he had to miss games and/or practices because of his duties at the paper, so I didn't know if I would have help from day to day.

Mike Quirk was a local chiropractor who played a lot of basketball for Chisholm High School. But football was Mike's sport and he excelled on the gridiron, both for the Bluestreaks and Moorhead State College. He basically worked with our low post players and I was pleased with our increased rebounding game. Mike was a banger under the hoop and he transferred this knowledge to our players to a point where he made bangers out of some of our low post kids.

Duane Erickson served as our college Financial Aid Officer and possessed a good athletic background, so I was happy to have him on the staff. This was a big advantage for the college with both coaches being members of the faculty. That meant the two of us were in touch with our players throughout the day.

Figure 39: Photo by Dick Varichak
Duane Erickson – Assistant BB Coach

Duane was not a talker like Schmitz or Anzelc, but could get his points over in his quiet, deliberate manner. He directed practices meticulously and wouldn't put up with slackers. He didn't say much on the bench, but the one time he did, he got me in trouble.

We were in a physical battle down at Brainerd against Brainerd State Junior College in a big conference basketball game. The two teams became rougher as the game progressed and I complained several times to no avail. After one battle under the boards, two of our players got slammed to the floor and were slow to get up. We were fortunate that neither player was seriously hurt, but just shaken up. I once again complained to the officials, but all I got in return was, "Go sit down Coach, and quit crying." I dutifully sat down again but as the action came past our bench, one of the officials stopped, looked at me and shouted, "Coach, now you got your "T!" He gave me the technical foul and I was stunned and asked him why. His reply was, "Do you want another one?" I sat back once again and kept my mouth shut for the remainder of the game, still wondering how come I got tagged with a technical. On the way home after the game, Duane sidled up to me and quietly stated, "Coach, I want to apologize to you for that technical you got tonight." Duane explained, "Actually, the official reacted when I asked him if he left his seeing-eye dog at home." That gave me quite a hearty chuckle and I think Duane was relieved that I was not upset over his actions.

Football gave me a little more freedom from hands-on coaching as I enjoyed three or four assistants who handled their part of the team's progress. I served as an assistant myself and aided Joe Milinovich, Art Malo, and Don Skoy in their head coaching stints. I was fortunate to have Art Malo come back and help me in my first year as head man. His football knowledge was invaluable for our staff planning on the offensive side of the ball. I had served as Art's offensive coordinator when he was the boss, so I wanted to have him direct my offense. Our only philosophical difference was in the passing game. Art believed that three things can happen when you throw a pass and two of them are bad – interception and incomplete. On the other hand, I believed the one good thing that can happen will bring a score or put a team back in the game. But he was an excellent coordinator and we had a lot of good times together.

Fifty-Five Years on the Bench

Figure 40: Photo by Dick Knable
Hibbing Cardinal Football Coaching Staff – 1983
Dick Varichak, Art Malo, Doug Schmitz, Terry Filippi

    Terry Filippi was another top-notch football mind and handled my defense. I remember one year when we had a dearth of big, strong defensive players. All we had was a lot of quickness, so Terry devised defensive maneuvers which had our smaller players criss-crossing on attack and believe me, we had opponent linemen highly confused on who they had to block. We knew our smaller linemen couldn't out-wrestle bigger and stronger opposition, so we ran away from them and raced to the ball carrier. Terry really made our defense the talk of the conference.

    I was very proud to have my son, Don, put in a stint as an assistant. He covered the defensive backs and did an extremely thorough job of teaching our D-backs. Having played a defensive back through high school and college, he was familiar with what we wanted to do and the players highly respected him.

    Bob Rolle, from Chisholm, was hired as our offensive coordinator in 1987 and I discovered he had an extremely fertile mind when it

Richard W. Varichak

came to putting the ball in play. He had a talented quarterback in Kyle Forsline, who he worked with on the Bluestreak staff. Forsline also had a couple of top-notch receivers in Darron "Irish" Riley and Jim Carlson. With this talented trio, Rolle instituted one of the best offenses we've had in years. In fact, in our home game, that year against Vermilion we rolled up 21 points in the first 8 minutes of the contest, thanks to the touchdown duo of Riley and Carlson. Vermilion, in the past, had pounded on us, and Rolle was out for blood. I ordered him to pull off the dogs and I could see the disappointment in his eyes. I told him that the current Vermilion squad was not the club who had administered big defeats on us. We did win 36-21 and probably could have scored 70 points, but we were not there to humiliate the opposition.

Figure 41: Photo by Al Higgins - HCC
Hibbing Cardinal Football Coaching Staff – 1988
Don Varichak, Mike Olson, Bob Rolle
Dick Varichak, Terry Filippi

Mike Olson was one of my football captains and a tough offensive and defensive lineman. He went on to play four-year ball at the University of Wisconsin-Superior and came back to help us with the offensive line. Mike was a good technician and our line play improved as he demanded fundamental skills. I was sorry to see him go and today he is an administrator with Little Falls High School.

Fifty-Five Years on the Bench

After my many years as a head coach, I was fortunate to finish up my coaching career on the assistant side of the bench. Most of it was spent with Doug Schmitz and this experience helped me truly understand the value and importance of this crucial coaching position.

Chapter 15: Junior College Football Was Fun

My introduction to junior college football came about while I was still playing for my Chisholm High School Bluestreaks. As a spectator, I watched the Hibbing Cardinals play in old Cheever Stadium, mostly on Thursday nights. Former Chisholm teammates dotted the Cardinal lineup each year and usually were instrumental in the team's gridiron success.

My chance to put on a Cardinal uniform came after a semester at UMD and seven months as an underground miner. Transferring to HJC for the 1950-51 year gave me an opportunity to get back to a sounder academic base and a chance to play college football. Joe Milinovich showed me how to play the game and made a running back out of me. We won the conference crown and the 1950 State Championship, whipping Worthington Junior College in the title game. Along the way, I played with ex-Chisholm teammates Frank Bay, Leo Hartman, Adrian Scaloni and Babe Altuvilla. It was a pleasure to play along with Dick Garmaker, Myrle Rice and Jerry Kepler from Hibbing, with Doug Lindahl and Dennis O'Brien from Keewatin and Nashwauk.

I came back to the Iron Range in the fall of 1963 to join the Hibbing Junior College faculty and to coach basketball and track. I was thrilled to be back "home" even though my beautiful Texan wife, Noka, thought she would eventually freeze to death. Although I was not contracted to coach football, Joe asked me to help out and pick up some more football coaching. I joined him and his assistant, Terry Carlson, but did very little hands-on coaching. Joe and Terry did most of the work while I just learned more about the game. When Joe and Terry retired, Hibbing hired a former North Dakota player and graduate, Art Malo. Art was hired as a counselor and took over a squad which had been down for a couple of years. Art asked me to help out as offensive coordinator and I accepted and looked forward to the new adventure.

In our first two years after I joined Malo's staff, we went from the outhouse to the penthouse with basically some of the same kids. In

Fifty-Five Years on the Bench

our first year, we had a lot of freshmen who were slow in adjusting to college football. We opened up our season with a 13-7 win over Normandale State Junior College which happened to be in their first year of their football program. We were delighted with the win because we didn't have many of those in the past but that was our only high spot of the year. We then dropped our next 7 games because we couldn't find a good mix between our offense and defense. My cousin, Jim Varichak, our quarterback, spent most of his time running for his life and our offensive game just deteriorated with each contest. We finally went to the old single wing offense which wasn't the answer to our woes and we were glad to see the season come to an end.

When we stored the uniforms away after the losing year, Coach Malo remarked, "The heck with this losing B.S. We're going out and get some football players." Malo was true to his word as we hit the recruiting trail with the goal to make our football program more competitive. We had some talented ball players returning and they would serve as good building blocks. Jim Varichak, Mike Zakula, Dan Moberg, Mike Raskovich, Wayne Perreault and Stu Mckie were college skilled players and would lead the 1971 Cardinals. We got Tom Ronchetti from Hibbing High School and made him a quarterback over the summer, converting him from a defensive back. Varichak, who quarterbacked the team last year went back to his defensive back slot and was very happy with the switch. Mike Zakula, who was our only offensive threat last season, finished up 13th in the nation in rushing, a $_{superb}$ job considering we lost 7 of 8 games and suffered from weak line play. We were blessed to receive Doug Schupp from Iron Mountain, Michigan, along with Stu Schley and Tom Cochenauer, a couple of defensive head hunters from Pennsylvania. Al McKibbon, a 6'4", 250-pound dynamo came in from Babbitt and from Nashwauk we got Joe Denucci, Bob Lucca, Bob Buescher, and Kenny Schmidtbauer, all outstanding linemen.

With a solid nucleus of pretty good football players, we made the journey to Bloomington to open the season against Normandale. Now in their second year of competition, this was a changed team, plus we had 5 starters out with injuries. Normandale shut us out 33-0 and left some

Richard W. Varichak

doubts in the minds of the coaching staff just how good we were. The tri-captains, Zakula, Moberg and Perrault, devised a killer drill for each Monday following a loss on Saturday. So two days after Normandale kicked our tails, the team went through this drill to start practice. After the drill, the players decided they were not going to lose again. Our kids came together, both on offense and defense, to win the next seven games and the conference championship.

    The key game for the crown came against Mesabi State Junior College and was played on the Buhl High School football field before a sell-out crowd. It was also the home turf of our lightning-quick running back, Mike Zakula, who had rushed for almost 800 yards in the preceding 8 games. The game was a defensive battle with both teams in a 3-3 deadlock late in the fourth quarter. With the ball on our 45 yard line, Mike took a quick pitch, skirted his left end and raced 55 yards for the only touchdown of the game and a 9-3 win. Jim Varichak clinched victory a few minutes later as he picked off a desperation Mesabi pass in the end zone to end the Norsemen threat. As we celebrated in the locker room, the players decided to throw the coaches in the showers. We were herded into the showers and were getting soaked while my son, Don, broke out in tears, thinking the team was mad and trying to hurt us. Cousin Jim Varichak went over to console him and allayed his fears by telling him they were having fun. I don't know if Don actually believed him but he did stop crying and was relieved that I was alright. All we had left on our schedule was a home game with Golden Valley and we disposed of them on a rainy, sloppy afternoon 15-3. The game was highlighted by a grand total of 16 fumbles, 10 by Golden Valley.

    Here we are, the State Championship game and we will be playing undefeated Normandale, down in Bloomington. We remembered the 33-0 white-washing they gave us on our opening game, also down in Bloomington. But at that time we had 5 players on the injured list that did not play, so I guess we had an excuse. We were all healthy now and on an eight game winning streak so we were ready to play. Unfortunately, Mother Nature played a dirty trick on us that night with the temperature at 17 degrees and the wind blowing fiercely cross field right in our face

Fifty-Five Years on the Bench

on the sideline. Defensive back Tom Cochenhauer called me over during pre-game warm-ups and said, "Coach, watch this." He then took a short run and slid for over 15 yards, showing me that the field resembled a skating rink. I told him, "Tom, the frozen field will affect Normandale, too." Boy was I wrong! The Normandale players changed into tennis shoes (we didn't have that option) and they enjoyed hot air fans behind their bench, something else we didn't have. The coaches decided to give our coaching shoes to our offensive backs so they would at least have some traction when we had the ball. Well, we were never in the ball game and lost 58-8. Under normal conditions, I believe we probably would have still lost, Normandale was that good, but I think the game would have been much closer.

Figure 42: Photo by Al Higgins - Hibbing State Junior College
1971 NJCC Champions
Front row: D. Schuppe, T. Cochenour, M. Raskovich, D. Robbins, W. Randolph.
Middle row: Coach Varichak, Coach Malo, R. Sarff, T. Nosan, A. Tervo, R. Deblack, L. Bruno, Coach Widmark
Back row: K. Schmidtbauer, T. Mrak, T. Baldwin, A. McKibbon, F. Zbacnik, B. Buescher, H. Brumbaugh, G. Spolarich, J. Varichak, S. McKie, K. Solars.

Richard W. Varichak

The next year I was appointed Men's Athletic Director, so my football coaching came to an end – for a while. When Art Malo took on some teaching duties a few years later, he also gave up the football job. For the next few years after Malo, we went through a succession of coaches who stayed only a year or two and then moved on. The Cardinals persuaded long time assistant, Terry Filippi, to take the 1982 team, which had been left with few football players and no recruiting by the former coach. The season was a disaster as the Cardinals went 0-8 and scored only one touchdown all year. At the end of the season, Terry said he couldn't continue as head coach but would stay on as an assistant. My son, Don, had just graduated from Hibbing High School and planned on attending Hibbing Community College to play both football and basketball. We hired Don Skoy, who had been a successful coach at Buhl High School, to head our down-trodden program. We also added Kenny Young, another successful coach who led the Nashwauk-Keewatin Spartans to several championships, as our defensive coordinator. I decided to get back in the football coaching picture along with Filippi – I would help Skoy with the offense and Terry would aid Young with the defense.

Don was our quarterback and safety, as a few of the players had to go both ways. We didn't have too many good college players on the squad. Besides Don, we had Mike Olson, Emil Renskowski, Keith Hukka, Don Quirk, and Mark Saccoman who would all qualify as bonafide college football talent. Renskowski was our 240-pound fullback who got those hard 3- and 4-yard gains. Quirk was our glue-fingered wide receiver, while Olson and Hukka were hard-nosed linemen. Saccoman, our pint-sized defensive safety was a tremendous hitter who sometimes had to be helped off the field after a devastating collision with a running back or blocker. Sometimes I had to hide his helmet so he couldn't get back into the action. You talk about dynamite in a small package!

Don Varichak, like his cousin, Jim Varichak, had to run for his life many times and took a lot of hard shots when carrying the ball on our veer offense. Our only win of the season came on a forfeit over

Fifty-Five Years on the Bench

Northland Community College when it was discovered they used an ineligible player.

Figure 43: Photo by Al Higgins - Hibbing CC
Hibbing Cardinal 1984 Tri-Captains
Don Varichak (14), Keith Hukka (71), Mike Olson (64)

Upon the completion of the season, Provost Orville Olson offered the position of head football coach to me for the following year. Former coaches, Skoy and Young, had decided to leave to pursue other interests. Terry and I had enjoyed the players, even though we had a losing season, so we decided to take the job. We had some of those good sophomores back but we were still short of being a competitive college football team. The seven or eight quality players went two-ways for us and Don also performed on kick-off and punt return teams. Art Malo

Richard W. Varichak

and Doug Schmitz also joined our coaching staff and the season proved to be enjoyable although we didn't win many games.

Prior to our first game, Don asked me to keep him at a defensive safety and give the quarterback job to a young freshman from Hinckley. I didn't see anything wrong with this decision and installed the freshman, Jody Anderson, as our starting Q-back. Anderson's inexperience showed early as we dropped our first two games to Brainerd and UM-Crookston. He was prone to throw into multiple coverages and suffered 7 interceptions through the first two games. In our third game, hosting Northland, we were suffering on offense and trailed at half-time 19-0. As we walked off the field, I was faced with a coaching revolt when Art Malo and Terry Filippi both approached me and declared, "If you don't put your son back at quarterback, we're going to hand in our whistles and retire. You've given Anderson more than enough time to produce and it's evident he can't cut it." I was a little stunned at this outburst, but in reality, I was thinking about making the change. When I informed Don that he was going back to quarterback for the second half, he wasn't too happy, but I think he saw it was better for the team. Of course, Anderson wasn't overjoyed with the decision and he left the team the following week.

With Don Varichak as the man over center, the Cardinals came back to score twice to narrow the margin to 19-14 going into the last few minutes remaining in the game. Don completed 12 of 15 passes and two touchdowns up to that point and they almost pulled the game out of the fire when the Cards drove down to the 5-yard line with one play left. Don's pass to a wide open receiver in the end zone was dropped and Hibbing went down to their 3rd straight loss, but we felt our quarterback problem was solved.

Once again, we were winless but were more competitive than in the past and we did play some good football. Our big problem was we did not have enough college caliber players. We were short on numbers and lacking in talent. Starting with the 1985 team, we started winning some recruiting wars. From 2-6 in 1985 we then produced 3-5 records for three years in a row and two second place finishes in the Northern

Fifty-Five Years on the Bench

Division. Our 1987 year looked promising as we opened up with three straight wins, including a last minute field goal by Jim Herold to defeat Brainerd 21-18 and a last second touchdown strike by Jon Spry to Don Polkinghorne for a 17-16 win over UM-Crookston. Then disaster! The following week against Fergus Falls, they picked us apart 42-13 to burst our bubble. We never did recover and finished the seasons with 5 defeats. From unproven statements analyzing our slump came the theory that some of our key players started on the party trail and were not physically and mentally ready to play college football.

The 1988 season started even more promising with a dozen sophomore returnees coming back from last year's team. We made some big recruiting gains which gave the coaching staff a faint hope for championship honors. We got the best quarterback on the Range from Chisholm, Kyle Forsline. The 6'2" sharpshooter not only had a rifle arm but was highly intelligent. To make use of his accurate arm, we had Darron "Irish" Riley and Jim Carlson on the receiving end of his passes. Riley, a 6'5" speedster was also a punt and kick-off returner, who ran several back for long gains and touchdowns. Carlson, from Askov-Sandstone High School, proved to be a sticky-fingered receiver giving the team a deep passing threat. One of the best offensive linemen on the team was Nick Skarich from Virginia who garnered All State honors and helped develop our running game, spearheaded by halfbacks Jim Puhek and Barry Sanders. The league proved to be super tough this year and we suffered 5 losses in our first 6 games, but the action was very competitive. We just didn't learn how to win yet!

We saved our best for last. We came alive to win our last two games of the season to finish up 3-5 and 2-1 in conference play, good for second place in the Northern Division. We first came alive offensively against Vermilion Community College, running up a 21-0 lead in the first 8 minutes of play. This was highlighted by a 68-yard punt return for a touchdown by Riley and then two touchdown passes to the big wide receiver. We took pity on the Ironmen the rest of the game and finally prevailed 36-21.

Richard W. Varichak

Figure 44: Photo by Hibbing Daily Tribune
Kyle Forsline backs up to pass as the Hibbing Cardinals went out a winner in their last game at Cheever Field, 16-7 over Itasca.

In our final contest of the year, we hosted Itasca Community College on a cold, windy, snowy evening. This would be the last game to be played in Cheever Stadium as they would move the field to the Community College grounds next seasons. The wind did affect both teams and we trailed at half-time by a slim 7-6 score. Jay Kitner, our punter, had a tough time getting the snap from Center on punt situations because we were with the wind and the strong breeze prevented the ball from getting back to him. I came up with a possible solution to this problem during our half-time meeting. I put our quarterback, Kyle Forsline, behind the center to take a direct snap and then turn and toss the ball back to Kitner who then could handle the ball. As we prepared to punt in third quarter action, with the wind again, we put this change in operation. Itasca, observing Forsline behind the center, came up to defend, leaving the field empty for a punt return. Just as we outlined, Forsline took the snap, tossed it to Kitner, who delivered a beautiful punt that went out of bounds on the Itasca 2-yard line. Two plays later, Itasca fumbled and we recovered on their 5-yard line. Forsline then kicked a field goal three plays later and we went out in front by a 9-7 margin. Once again the same situation came up with fourth down for us on our 45-yard line. Forsline, once again, took his position behind the center and

Fifty-Five Years on the Bench

the Vikings were really confused and were hesitant to drop into punt return formation. Kitner came through with another fine punt with the ball again going out-of-bounds on their 11-yead line. Another Itasca fumble gave us the ball near the end zone and we added another touchdown for a well-deserved 16-7 win. The players awarded me the game ball and agreed they never saw that strategy on our punting situation work so well.

That was my last game as the Cardinal head football coach and it was with one of my favorite teams. Kyle Forsline finished the year with over 1,000 yards passing and 11 touchdowns. He proved to be one of the most athletic quarterbacks in my coaching tenure and what a great individual to have on the squad! Jim Carlson led the team with 23 pass completions and 5 touchdowns while Darron Riley caught 21 passes for 438 yards and 6 touchdowns. On the defensive side of the field, Mike Moehrke made All-State and All-Conference as a defensive back along with Trey Hagan and Dan Arnberg, two hard-hitting linebackers.

I think we built a good base for future Hibbing teams. Dale Heffron came in 1990 and led the Cardinals to a State crown and a bowl game in 1991 where the team charged to an 11-1 record. The only defeat came in the Bowl game in Iowa where the Cards lost 38-36 in the final minutes. Hibbing placed two players on the Junior College All-American squad. Scott Antonutti from Esko was our clutch pass receiver for two years. He did not have blazing speed, but owned the best pair of hands I've ever seen on a receiver. He always found an open spot in the defensive secondary and when we needed that crucial first down, our quarterback knew who to look for.

Scott was a joy to coach and I knew he would make an excellent teacher and coach. After another good two years of football at Jamestown College in North Dakota, he taught and coached at Fosston High School and now serves as the head girls' basketball coach at Esko High School. Bryce Bogenheimer played his high school football at Moose Lake and performed as an offensive lineman for the Cardinals. Standing at 6'1" and 255-pounds, he used his strength and speed to bolster our athletic line, spearheading an outstanding offensive attack. Both Anto-

Richard W. Varichak

nutti and Bogenheimer were prime examples of what small school athletes can accomplish through hard work and dedication to their goals. Also, a solid reason why we go on coaching – they make it fun!

Football at Hibbing would be played for another 15 years through the tenures of Rick Tintor, Todd Hickman and Kurt Zuidmulder. After some problems with a few out-of-state players, the program was discontinued in 2006. I was sorry to see the sport dropped and felt it left a hole in the athletic makeup of the college. But I have many pleasant memories that community college football afforded me and the super kids who played for us.

Figure 45: Photo by Dale Heffron -
Hibbing CC
Scott Antonutti
Wide Receiver
1991 Junior College All-American

Figure 46: Photo by Al Higgins -
Hibbing CC
Bryce Bogenheim
Offensive Guard
1991 Junior College All-American

Chapter 16: Would You Coach a Relative?

When I prepared for a coaching profession, I never thought about being involved in a coach-player relationship with one of my relatives. This relationship actually first happened when at age 14, I coached my younger brother, Kenny, in Midget softball. Even at my young age I was devising practice drills and looking forward to mapping out offensive strategy with my young softballers. Another brother came under my supervision nine years later when I came home from Japan while serving in the U.S. Navy. I was asked to head the Chisholm Midget baseball team and since I was home for a month, I accepted the challenge. My brother, George Varichak (Butch) held down the third base position and was the leading hitter on the team. It was an enjoyable month and I found out that coaching a brother was a lot of fun and a fulfilling experience. Butch came into my coaching life again in 1963 when he decided to attend Hibbing Junior College and play basketball for me. Then five years passed before I inherited another Varichak to play both football and basketball. Jim Varichak, my cousin, came in from Chisholm where he was a solid performer for the Bluestreaks in both sports. My son, Don Varichak, decided he wanted to play community college football for me and his participation was a highlight of my coaching career. Actually, I coached Don in Little League baseball when he was 13 years old so I already had a coaching life with him. Many coaches do not like to coach their offspring and will quit the business rather than be involved. I found the experience wonderful and enjoyed every minute that I had with Don. This feeling was also prevalent with all the other loved ones whom I had the pleasure to coach.

After Don left, my nephew, Kenneth Varichak, Jr., came in from Kittitas, Washington. The son of my brother, Ken Varichak, he was a tough linebacker for Kittitas High School and led them to the State playoffs. Very under-sized for a college linebacker, he got by on a hard work ethic, plus performing on a small school competitive level.

Fifty-Five Years on the Bench

Kyle Jacobson and Travis Varichak came under my coaching hands in 2000 when they were 10 years old and participants in our Nashwauk-Keewatin boys' basketball summer camp. Kyle is the son of my daughter Vikki and Travis is the son of my other daughter Pam. Both youngsters showed promising athletic competence, although Travis discontinued playing sports while Kyle went on to play high school football and wrestle for the Hibbing Bluejackets. He later wrestled for the Vikings at Itasca Community College. Beau Jacobson (another grandson), also played for me at Coach Dick Larson's Bluejacket summer camp. Beau went on to play varsity basketball and football with the Bluejackets a couple years later, followed by performing in the lead position of quarterback with the Hibbing Community College Cardinals.

My girls finally came into the picture with Shawna Varichak as a 6th and 8th grader. Shawna, the daughter of Don Varichak, played on the Washington 6th grade squad, on my 8th grade team, and then three years on the Hibbing H.S. varsity squad. Her basketball career was ended in her junior year of high school with an ACL injury. Her sister, Taylor Varichak, first played for me as a 4th and 5th grader and then as a C-team player in 9th grade. Vanessa Jacobson (Vikki's daughter) played only one year for me as 6th grade basketball player, then decided to be a cheerleader. I think she missed her calling! She did join the cross-country team in her senior year of high school in addition to participating in cheerleading.

Another daughter from the Jacobson family not only played for me in the Bluejacket girls' basketball program, but went on to perform two years at Hibbing Community College and one year at the University of Minnesota – Morris before a volleyball injury took her off the court. Lindsay was a member of my "Fab 9," the nine girls who started with me and Doug in 7th grade and stayed with the program until graduation from Hibbing H.S. Lindsay was a two-sport starter in both volleyball and basketball in high school and community college. As the captain of her college volleyball team, she led her team to a 3rd place finish in the national tournament. She concentrated on only volleyball with her one year at UM-Morris. A coach's dream!

Richard W. Varichak

My very first venture in the coaching field involved my 12-year old brother, Kenny Varichak. Being an active participant on the Roosevelt playground in Chisholm's recreation program, I was approached by Swede Pergol, our Recreation Director, to coach the Roosevelt Midget Softball team. Kenny was the third baseman and a pretty good infielder. There wasn't much coaching going on at this level. I was responsible for making out the lineup, holding practice sessions, and reporting game scores upon completion of the contest. I had enough softball and baseball knowledge to give out a few tips to the players and was surprised I was a little more knowledgeable than the team members. Having played the infield myself, I passed on certain information on how to hold the glove while receiving throws and fielding ground balls. This was really important information to Kenny as he had some problems in fielding ground balls. The biggest job in relating information was to help players understand the game more completely- position playing, when and where to throw the ball and to which base – all skills and game knowledge that is important to play the game properly. The coaching fever probably started at this time!

Figure 47: Photo by Propotnick Studios
Ken Varichak
Softball third baseman on my Roosevelt playground team in 1945.

The second brother to come under my coaching umbrella was George Varichak, better known to all of us as "Butch." I still don't know how he acquired that nickname but nobody told me why I was called "Sonny" either. I am eight years older than my brother and according to our dad I was Butch's idol all through my high school career. I believe this affection was a positive factor in our coach-player relationship years later.

Fifty-Five Years on the Bench

As detailed in preceding chapters, I first had the opportunity to coach Butch while he was playing Midget baseball in our home town of Chisholm, Minnesota. I was in the military, 23 years old, and home between Navy assignments when I got the coaching position. Although he had some heart problems, he was allowed to participate in baseball but was unable to compete in football and basketball. He was finally cleared medically to play all three sports in his high school junior year. He decided to pass up college after a good athletic two years with the Chisholm Bluestreaks and went to Seattle with the family. I finally convinced him to go to Hibbing Junior College in 1963 where he could get his first two years of school and also play basketball for me. He followed through with his decision and I found him a joy to coach. He did tell me that he wouldn't call me Mr. Varichak (it was awkward for him), but he did call me Sonny. At 24 years of age, Butch started for me at center although he was only 5'11". His previous participation in a tough Seattle summer basketball league for several years gave him a load of experience and the ability to play a physical game with anybody. He was not a high scorer for me, but his play on defense and rebounding value was very instrumental in the success of our team.

Figure 48: Photo by Propotnick Studios
George Varichak
Starting center on Cardinal basketball team at age 24. Honor to coach a brother.

He went on to get his B.S. degree from the University of Washington, bypassed a teaching career, and went to work with the Seattle Recreation Department. After realizing he could not advance professionally any further in the recreation field, he began employment with Boeing Aircraft as a buyer. He retired from Boeing and moved to Stevensville,

Richard W. Varichak

Montana where he worked with several companies. He also ended his athletic playing days, finally giving up on softball and basketball early in his fifties. Even in his fifties, he was a big factor in his teams' successes — he could still play! He also enjoyed a few years of substitute teaching at Stevensville and displayed his versatility, teaching physical education, social studies, and even stepped in as a band instructor. Will wonders never cease!

One of his big moments playing for me at the college was an exploding score night. We were at Gogebic Junior College in Ironwood, Michigan playing an always tough opponent. Butch was hotter than a pistol in the first half, pumping in 23 points in the first 20 minutes. We could hear the Gogebic coach in a nearby locker room berating his club. One of his comments was, "Can't anyone of you jokers stop that old grandpa playing center for them?" This brought a chorus of laughs from our team plus some back-slapping from Butch's teammates. He ended up with 27 points as we won in easy fashion. Butch summed up his feelings on our relationship as coach and player with the following observation.

"It is an experience that has many facets and emotional ups and downs that at times tests your resolve. I have been fortunate to play sports for Coach Sonny and it has been an extremely rewarding and enjoyable experience. His coaching techniques are always positive and instructive. Many of his techniques and ideas are transferable to life lessons. The best part of having a relative as a coach is that relationship never ends and for the rest of your life you have that coach and mentor in your corner. It has been an extreme pleasure and honor to have Coach Sonny as a brother and coach."

My big wish for my brother was to see him go into the field of education. He would have made an excellent teacher and coach. His personality, love of athletics, and the ability to reach young people would have given us another very good educator and athletic leader. But his big contribution was to make my coaching profession one of a labor of love. Thank you, brother!

My cousin, Jimmy, the youngest of three brothers, all solid athletes, is the son of my namesake, Uncle Dick Varichak. Jim followed his

Fifty-Five Years on the Bench

oldest brother, also named Dick Varichak, to get his first two years of college education at Hibbing Community College. Dick, after two years of junior college football finished up at the University of Minnesota – Duluth where he earned his teaching degree and played two years for the UMD football team. Middle brother, Tom Varichak, after a great athletic career at Chisholm High School, played four years of football at North Dakota State University and also garnered his teaching credentials. He never got to a classroom though. He started a business venture with Jerry Janezich, a close friend who also had a teaching diploma, and now they are co-owners of Tom and Jerry's Bar and Lounge in Chisholm, Minnesota.

Figure 49: Photo by Propotnick Studio
Jim Varichak
Quarterback and defensive back in football, Guard on the basketball team, 1970-72 HSJC Cardinals.

Jim followed in the footsteps of his two older brothers and was an all-around athlete at Chisholm High School. I was pleased to get him at Hibbing State Junior College where I wanted him to play both football and basketball. He stepped in as our quarterback in his freshman year and hated the experience. We had one of our down football seasons, winning our opening game and then losing the last seven games. Jim's problem (among others) came on offense as he was always running for his life and trying to direct our ineffective attack. Our offensive line proved to be inadequate to operate as a college unit and our defense seemed to be a step slower in trying to catch opposition runners.

The following year we were fortunate to get Tom Ronchetti from Hibbing H.S. to take over the quarterback slot, thus releasing Jim to go to a defensive safety position which he loved. I had to take Ronchetti

Richard W. Varichak

over the summer and teach him how to play as a quarterback. Tom originally was a wide receiver and defensive back in high school. Because of his athletic prowess he made the switch without any problem and led our 1971 gridders to an 8-2 record and the Northern Division championship. What a ride! From the outhouse to the penthouse in one year. Of course, the answer was to get better players and that we did. Jim was a tough defensive back and took no guff from opponents. In our road game against Fergus Falls, he complained to me that a Fergus player was continually holding him on punt returns. I told him to tell the official, which he did, to no avail. He decided to solve the problem himself and before we knew it, the grabber on the other team had to leave the game with a dislocated elbow. Jim certainly took care of the problem.

In our championship conference game against Mesabi C.C., he came through with a last minute pass interception in the end zone to preserve our 9-3 win.

Although undersized for a college forward, Jim won a starting position for me in his year and a half of community college basketball. He decided to drop from the basketball team in his sophomore year because I don't think he was having fun again. Although I hated to lose him, I respected his decision because I always preached that one should not participate if one was not enjoying the sport. Jim was a dedicated athlete and he gave me a lot of pleasure as his coach in both sports. He eventually went on to Moorhead State University to play some more football and received his teaching degree. After serving as a teacher and principal, he now occupies the chair of Superintendent of Schools for the Chisholm School District. He proved to be a winner!

Donald Gene Varichak came into this world in our second year in Hibbing and was only a few weeks old when he saw his first college basketball game. From this auspicious beginning, he developed into a competitive, intelligent athlete who gave me some of my greatest moments in coaching. I know some of my coaching colleagues discontinue their duties when an offspring becomes eligible to play for them. I had the opposite philosophy and looked forward to be involved with Don as a coach. We got together in Don's 13th year when I became his Little

Fifty-Five Years on the Bench

League coach. It was his second year playing for Erickson Lumber under Al Nyberg, his head coach. Unfortunately, Al became ill and I had to assume the head job. We were fortunate to get some good kids who knew baseball and we went all the way to the finals where we lost in the championship game. Don was my shortstop and batted second in my lineup. He scored a lot of runs because hitting third was Scott Sandelin (UMD hockey coach today) who could hit a ball a mile and led our team in runs batted in. At this young age, Don displayed a smooth fielding technique and was a tough player to get out at the plate. I could see he was going to be a pretty good athlete, and at a young age he proved to be an organizer. Growing up in a great neighborhood, he was the catalyst in organizing football, basketball, and baseball games with his friends and playmates. I can still remember how he used to announce to me that it was time to go out in the yard and play catch. When it was

Figure 50: Photo by Al Higgins - HCC
Don Varichak
One of the great pleasures in my coaching career – to coach my son.

baseball season, he would bring his glove, ball, and my glove and walk out to the back yard. It was the same scene with a football and a basketball. He didn't have to say a word. I knew what he wanted.

Don finished his high school athletic career at Hibbing High by being the lone male senior athlete to letter in three sports – football, basketball, and baseball. Although getting correspondence from some four year schools, he chose to spend his first two years at Hibbing Community College. I was his head coach in his sophomore year and

Richard W. Varichak

although we didn't have a lot of wins in his two seasons, he proved to be one of the few pure college football players to perform for me. He seldom came off the field because of his versatility, operating as our quarterback on offense, safety on defense, while pulling duty on both punt and kicking teams. My wife, Noka, pleaded with me to pull him off some of those teams but I think Don would have been disappointed if I heeded her request. He finished his community college football career by attaining All-Conference honors on both offense and defense, a feat accomplished only by two players playing community college football. This was quite an honor for a player who played on a team that won only two games in two years.

He played for Doug Schmitz during the basketball season and was a member of one of Doug's best teams in his sophomore year. Although not a starter, he turned out to be a valuable rotation player who could serve as a forward or guard. It didn't seem to bother him to come off the bench because he knew he would get quality minutes of play. His floor game and outside shooting skill gave the Cardinals valuable reserve strength.

The fact that I was a professional coach sometimes did not make an impression on Don. If his other coaches had a little different philosophy than mine on certain skills, offense, defense, etc., he sometimes agreed with his current coach. This didn't bother me because there is always varied thinking on coaching agendas or plans and it isn't a matter of being right or wrong. I remember one instance when discussing the end of a fast break situation. My practice was different than his high school coach, Gary Addington. His remark which ended our discussion, in defense of Addington's way was, "Oh Dad, you don't know what you're talking about." Me – a coach for over 30 years – I didn't know what I was talking about! What a son! This brought out a lot of laughter from the family. Actually, I believe Don brought out more love of coaching for me and motivated me to bring my professionalism to a much higher level.

One of the coaching surprises of my life came in the form of my nephew, Kenneth Varichak wanting to attend HCC and play football for

Fifty-Five Years on the Bench

me. Kenneth was a graduate of Kittitas High School, a small high school located in the state of Washington. He was a tough, scrappy linebacker who helped get his team to the state playoffs. His father, my brother Kenny Varichak, played softball for me when he was 12 years old and figured I still knew what I was doing in the field of coaching. He sent me game film on Ken's state playoff game and, I will admit, Ken looked pretty good. On the other hand, I had to take into account he was only 5'7" and 160 pounds. The problem here was he was vastly undersized for a college linebacker, but I would have to see him in action.

Ken did enroll at Hibbing and lived with us for the school year. When football practice began, I knew he would have a tough time getting playing minutes. He just didn't have the size and quickness for college level action, especially at a linebacker position. He was a hard worker and was not afraid to hit people. I liked his enthusiasm and dedication to his practice skills but he was still over-matched by some of our big people. In our first game of the year, we romped over St. Paul Bible 48-6 and I had a chance to use him later in the game. He did well in his few minutes of play but got pushed around at times. His football career came to an end the following week when he suffered a painful ankle injury which put him out of commission for an extended period of time. We both decided that he could stay with the team as a manager and this worked out for both of us. For Kenneth, it gave him a college football experience and a year of college credits. We also had the opportunity to enjoy our nephew and cousin for nine months.

My three grandsons spent only a week with me as participants in a couple of boys' basketball camps. Beau Jacobson was in my first camp run by Bluejacket coach Dick Larson. As a member of the teaching staff of the camp, we were assigned a team to take part in the 5-on-5 scrimmages. I was lucky to get some talented players on my squad who would eventually dot our college roster years later. Players like Spinner Aune, Rob Bigelow, and Jeremy Fleming joined Beau to pace our team to the camp championship. Beau came off the bench for me and was an effective low post banger and was my best defensive player. He was a coach's dream because of his work ethic and ability to execute his duties.

Richard W. Varichak

His lack of size and quickness would keep him from gaining a starting position on the high school team, but he did play an important part coming off the bench for the Bluejackets. He definitely is the type of athlete who makes coaching fun.

Kyle Jacobson and Travis Varichak were enrolled in our Nashwauk-Keewatin camp as 10-year olds. Both were prospective varsity athletes and possessed good basketball skills. When our 5-on-5 competition started, I was lucky to get both of them on my team. We ran away from the other teams as Kyle and Travis dominated play. Travis was the smoother of the two and a better shooter. Kyle was a physical standout who pretty well dominated the low post play. The other coaches did complain about me getting the two "studs," but of course I had nothing to do with team selections. (Ha! Ha!). Travis did not follow up with his basketball play and in my estimation, probably would have been a starter for Coach McDonald and the Chisholm Bluestreaks. Kyle gravitated to the more physical activities and earned athletic letters in football and wrestling for the

Figure 52: Photo by Tom Lindstrom
Beau Jacobson
1992 Hibbing HS Basketball Camp

Figure 51: Photo by Enstrom Studios
Kyle Jacobson
Nashwauk-Keewatin 1999 Basketball Camp

Fifty-Five Years on the Bench

Bluejackets. He was also dominating in the sport of Karate. Kyle continued his participation in wrestling at Itasca Community College. Beau went on to get his two-year start at HCC where he also quarterbacked the Cardinal football team. All three were positive contributors to my coaching life even though I had them only for a short period of time. Time well spent for Coach V.

Shawna and I joined hands when she entered 6th grade at Washington Elementary school. In fact, I had two grand-daughters in the starting lineup that year as her cousin Vanessa Jacobson was the other forward. Shawna was still growing and was a little slow afoot but did exhibit a nice shooting touch. I could see a future low post performer, so we worked on some moves to help her offense. She was a quick learner although her strength at this age was her rebounding game.

We next touched base when she convinced me to coach her 8th grade team. We had enough girls to form two teams, so I asked Dave Ongaro to handle one team while I directed the other club. Shawna, along with some of the more talented teammates, made up my "blue" team while Dave took the lesser talented kids on the "white" team. I could see Shawna was going

Figure 53: Photo by Chisholm Tribune
Travis Varichak
Nashwauk-Keewatin 1999 Basketball Camp

Figure 54: Photo by Tom Lindstrom
Shawna Varichak
6th grade BB 1998-99
HHS Varsity BB 2001-02

150

Richard W. Varichak

to be one of the taller girls, so she stepped in as my starting center. Again, she still lacked a little quickness but still had her good shooting eye. She led our 8th graders to a respectable 18-6 record and although not a big scorer, she usually controlled the boards. Because of her asthmatic condition she needed periods of rest, but while she was on the floor she gave 100% effort. Shawna possessed unusual court sense for an 8th grader and these talents won her a starting position on the varsity as a freshman. Shawna Bear (my favorite name for her) continued to start for the Bluejackets until her junior year when she tore her ACL which ended her basketball career. Fortunately, she could fall back on her volleyball talent. After starring for Hibbing High School for four years, she took her talents to St. Scholastica to become one of the Saints most valuable players. With Shawna, I found coaching girls again could be loads of fun.

My Vanessa Louise played only one year for me at Washington Elementary as she and Shawna led our team to the city championship. She did not have the basketball skill work which benefitted my other grand-daughters so she was a little inexperienced in her year of competition. What she lacked in basic skill she made up for in her demanding physical play and defensive strength. She was always "in the face" of opponents and although drawing some personal fouls in her endeavors, she definitely made her opponent uneasy and shook up. In one of our games with Jefferson Elementary, she had been her usual physical self and at half-

Figure 55: Photo by Tom Lindstrom
Vanessa Jacobson
6th grade BB 1998-99

time one of the officials came over to me and declared that Vanessa could not play anymore. I wanted to know how he could make such a decision and he explained that the opposing coach told him that he was

Fifty-Five Years on the Bench

to keep her from playing because she was too "rough." I loudly informed the official (a young college student) that "nobody tells me who I can or cannot play and that includes that nincompoop coach of the other team." The startled official went over to the opposing coach, delivered my message, and Vanessa played the rest of the game. I later apologized to Mrs. Sue Moody, the opposing coach, but had to refresh her on the rules of competitive basketball. Vanessa decided that basketball was not her cup of tea but stayed with athletics as a hockey and wrestling cheerleader and cross-country runner.

Taylor Varichak was my little manipulator. She was in fourth grade when she convinced me to coach her team. Over at our house one day at the beginning of basketball season, she complained to her grandmom, Noka, that if their coach did not show up again for practice, the school was going to drop the program. She waited for me to come home to turn on the waterworks and with tears streaming down her cheeks, gave me the same sad tale she told Noka. I then told her, "Baby, I will be at your next practice and if he doesn't show up, I will be your coach." And that's how I became the Washington Wolves 4th grade coach. In addition, I also took the reins of the 5th grade team so I now would be coaching double-header games. Taylor had inherited the soft shooting touch from her dad, Don Varichak, and was a pretty knowledgeable basketball player for a 10-year old. She had a couple of talented teammates in the persons of Chris Nyberg and Rachel Miesbauer. Those three did most of the scoring and were easily the core of the team. On my 5th grade outfit I had Kate Lange and Allie Jaynes and that was the extent of that grade's talent. After Taylor and her crew finished their game, I took them and placed

Figure 56: Photo by Emily Law
Taylor Varichak
C-team BB, 2007-08
4th & 5th Grade Basketball

the three on the 5th grade squad to go with Kate and Allie. Needless to say, with that combination, we won both city championships with 5-1 records in each grade. Taylor's advanced skills reflected the time her Dad put in with her on one-on-one practices. Up to 8th grade she hesitated to drive to the basket, depending instead on her outside shooting game. It was only with her 8th grade team and participation on the C-team that she developed her driving game. I knew that she would see considerable playing time in her sophomore year. She surprised us all by deciding not to play basketball anymore and concentrate on volleyball. She just wasn't having fun anymore and I believed that when I opted to quit coaching it may have played a part in her decision. Once again, another member of my family made coaching a fulfilling and enjoyable job. Thanks Taylor!

Delightful grand-daughter, Lindsay Jacobson, took up the longest time of my coaching experience. Starting with our 7th grade team and extending through her senior year on the varsity, Lindsay and I were together as coach and player. There were only a couple weeks in her 9th grade year that she was under a different coach on the C-team. It didn't take long to realize that she was B-team material so she was back under my supervision very quickly. Lindsay was an extremely hard worker and put in many hours to sharpen her skills. She was an excellent shooter and possessed a high degree of court sense. She was not very quick so didn't drive to the hoop as often as we would have liked, but when she did she was effective.

Figure 57: Photo by Tom Lindstrom
Lindsay Jacobson
7th grade – Varsity BB
2001-2007

She was an intelligent player and used this intellect to compensate for her lack of quickness. One of her strengths was reflected in her consistent

Fifty-Five Years on the Bench

level of play. Although not usually our highest scorer, she did everything else on a positive scale. A standing joke between us developed when I wanted to address her from the bench while she was on the floor. If I wanted to just relay basic information, I would get her attention by shouting, "Lindsay, etc., etc.; but if she made a mental or physical mistake, which didn't happen often, my loud voice would reverberate, "Lindsay Mae!" The inclusion of her middles name (named after my mother) told her I was not happy with her mistake.

Lindsay went on to a basketball and volleyball experience for two years at Hibbing Community College. She was a starter in both sports and gained All-Conference honors in both activities. She became more of a scorer as a college basketballer and an extremely effective right side hitter on the volleyball court at HCC. Between high school and college, she was an instrumental player on seven state tournament teams. As Captain of her college volleyball team, she helped lead them to a 3rd place finish at the NJCAA National Tournament. She also proved to be a top-notch defensive star on the volleyball court. This skill enabled her to win a starting Libero slot on the University of Minnesota-Morris volleyball squad after her graduation as one of the three junior college transfers on the team. A serious back injury received during a volleyball tournament near the end of the season took her out of competition and off the court permanently.

She has made my coaching life a memorable and satisfying experience and states her feelings about our relationship in the following comments, "Out of all of the people whose life has been made better by my grandpa's kindness, I feel as if he has been the most caring toward me. My basketball coach since seventh grade, he truly has been to every one of my games. Whenever I wanted to shoot hoops, he was always there to take me to a gym or park and correct my technique. I sincerely believe that there isn't a more caring person in the world than my grandfather." Do you blame me for shedding some tears when you hear those words from a player/granddaughter? Thank you, Lindsay Mae!

Richard W. Varichak

When our grandson Cole Varichak opted to play 5th grade tackle football, I persuaded his dad, Don, to take the head coaching position for his team. I also agreed to help as an assistant coach, much to the dismay of my wonderful wife. But outside of a couple of rainy game days, the experience was positive for me, although the road trips to Cohasset, Deer River and Coleraine were a little tiresome.

Cole proved to be a very capable tight end who liked contact and was effective as a defensive end. In his final game of the season, he contributed to fine defensive play with twenty tackles. He still has to develop his pass-catching skills, but I feel that will come about as he gets older. He seemed to be pleased with the addition of Grandpa V. on the coaching staff and it gave me the opportunity to work with him on a one-to-one basis. I look forward to seeing him playing varsity football in a few years.

Figure 58: Photo by Tom Lindstrom
Cole Varichak
5th grad Football – Lincoln Elementary School - 2011

Dr. Vikki Lynne Varichak Jacobson was never one of my players, but she and I shared athletic memories which deserve mention in this chapter. Of course, she was an avid fan of my teams and probably saw more contests than anyone her age. In our conversation about the writing of this book, she remembered four situations in which her experiences in my coaching tenure were extremely notable.

I was in the habit of taking my children to out of town games and I think they enjoyed the experience. I took Vikki along on our game with Mesabi State Junior College in Virginia in 1969 when I had one of my best teams. The game was hard fought on both sides and we enjoyed an 11-point lead with just a few minutes left. At this point, a scuffle broke out with Jim Miskulin, from my team, and Don Lein, of Mesabi. Both

Fifty-Five Years on the Bench

benches erupted and fights broke out all over the floor. I rushed out to pull Frank Russ, my big scorer, away from the fighting when a Mesabi student sucker punched me in the face and down I went. I faintly remember Dan Poupard, from the Mesabi team, retaliate by punching the student who hit me and standing over me until our center, Tom Tintor, could pick me up and escort me to the sidelines. Vikki (12 years old), was terrified and began to cry when she realized that I was not fully conscious. This was the part of athletics that I did not want her to remember.

Her second strong memory also was basketball connected and, once again, was not positive. She accompanied the team and me to Ironwood, Michigan for our game with Gogebic Junior College. It was a rough game and the officials had lost some control over the action. Both coaches had a few complaints about the officiating and my temper finally got the best of me. One of the refs ejected our John Hughes after John accidentally threw the ball in his face. He handled John

Figure 59: Photo by John Peterson
Dr. Vikki Varichak Jacobson
BB ball girl 1960-62
BB statistician 1975-76
Football statistician 1987-88, 1990

pretty rough and pushed him to the sidelines. My next step was to grab the official by his shirt and shout, "Don't you dare touch my players!" As a result, of course, he threw me out of the game amid a lot of pushing and shoving from the Gogebic fans. I pulled my team off the floor and forfeited the game to the Sampsons – they were ahead 81-61 anyway. We got fined $50 by the Minnesota Community College Board for the action. Once again, my daughter saw athletics at its low level and I thought maybe I shouldn't bring her any more of my games on the road.

Richard W. Varichak

When she became a student at Hibbing Community College, she qualified for work study status. Naturally, I got her on my staff so she could work for her father. Oh! Was she happy! But that didn't last long. I don't think she was overjoyed when her duties were explained. A big part of her football duties was to handle the laundering of uniforms. Our school had their own washer and dryer and her responsibility was to get those uniforms nice and clean before the next game. Games were played on Saturday afternoon and the wet, smelly, dirty uniforms were taken off that day, thrown in a pile, waiting to be laundered on Monday morning. This was the day that Vikki dreaded each week. The uniforms now had lain around for 48 hours and the smell was overpowering! What Vikki had to do now was to handle all these uniforms without fainting, vomiting, or running out of the room. When she described her "work technique" she told me she learned exactly how long she could hold her breath. Her general comment – "Thanks a lot, daddy."

Her final notable adventure was also football-oriented when we enjoyed one of our best teams ever with Dale Heffron, our head coach, who turned out to be quite a loose cannon. Our opening game was a home affair with the game to be played in Nashwauk. Heffron announced that he was going to try and break the national passing record against our opponent, a weak St. Paul Bible eleven. In order to be eligible for a national record, the game stats have to be perfect. Unfortunately, this meant bringing my daughter, an experienced football statistician, out of retirement. So I went to Vikki to tell her that I needed her to take the stats for the game. 100% accuracy was required since this would be national news, so there was no one else I trusted for that. Her problem was that she was 8 ½ months pregnant, big as a house, and her doctor had told her not to leave town as the birth would be very soon. (It took her 70 minutes to deliver her last child so the doctor was serious about staying close to the hospital.) I assured her that we always have an ambulance on hand for each game. I don't know if that truly inspired her, but she never says no to her father's requests. (She teases me about missing the sensitivity gene with this request.)

Fifty-Five Years on the Bench

Vikki came to the game and found she was unable to navigate the ladder that led to the press box, so she had to take the stats from the stands, using her typical technique of talking into a tape recorder, never taking her eyes off the ball. With our powerhouse team and the weak opposition, Heffron got his wish and set the national record in our 81-6 win. My pregnant girl got every stat down perfectly and it was duly certified by the National Junior College Athletic Association and the National Collegiate Athletic Association.

Vikki's perspective of that game is a bit different than mine. As she describes it, "The stands were cold, hard and very uncomfortable when you are sitting through the longest game in the history of football. When your team uses a passing play every single down of the game, the clock stops a lot. And then it started to rain, and I'm thinking, 'Are you kidding me?' Only for my dad would I do such a thing." As a reward for her loyalty to her father she gave birth to a beautiful baby boy a few days later. What a gal!

Chapter 17: My Solid Six

With 55 years of coaching adventures under my belt, I knew when I began this book that I would have some outstanding experiences, teams and individuals to write about. As mentioned in past chapters, my Evant girls' basketball team was a unique group, as was the Fab nine Hibbing girls. I also must say that there is another group of young ladies who stands out in memory and gives me a warm feeling every time I look back on their relationship with me.

In my last year of teaching at Hibbing Community College, the women's basketball program fell into my lap. The original contract called for head football coach, Dale Heffron, to take over the women's program and I was hired to be his assistant. Our football season ended with a bowl game defeat in Iowa, but Heffron did not make it back to Hibbing. It seems there was an all-out brawl when the game ended and Heffron suffered a head injury. We never heard a word from him and I was then approached to take over the head job. I naturally accepted and convinced my daughter-in-law to take the assistant job. The arrangement worked out for both me and Tammy, who was a teacher at Washington Elementary. I already had a full teaching load for the quarter and I wouldn't get credit overload. So we arranged for Tammy to get the pay and I'm sure this helped Don and Tammy financially.

When practice began, we welcomed seven girls, all freshmen. Six were pretty good ball players and one was a mother with a young baby. Tammy Ricci from Nashwauk-Keewatin joined the squad a few days later and she and Teresa Burton (the mother) made up our bench contingent. Hibbing Bluejackets provided Becky Koslowski and Lisa Caldwell, while ex-Bluestreak Gina Quirk gave us low post strength. Char Omdahl came in from Mesabi East and proved to be our leading scorer. Another sharpshooter was Julie Wickstrom from Barnum, and our little pint-sized shooting guard, Michel Dicklich was a former cage star from Northwestern High School in Wisconsin. Later in the season, Tammy Thielen and

Fifty-Five Years on the Bench

Jennifer Baker came aboard but neither stayed too long. Thielen, standing 6'2" played in only one game and decided basketball was too much running. Baker, Burton and Ricci each played in only 8 games while the top six played in every contest. Quirk missed two games because of illness, the other five logged in all 20 games.

Our season was not a success in the win-loss record. We defeated Itasca three times and won two games from Rainey River on forfeits

Figure 60: Photo by Carol Lind – HCC – 1991-1992
Back row: Tina Nesgoda (mgr), Tammy Varichak, Dick Varichak
Middle row: Jennifer Baker, Char Omdahl, Lisa Caldwell, Julie Wickstrom, Michel Dicklich
Front row: Gina Quirk, Shawna Varichak (ball girl), Becky Koslowski

because they used an ineligible player. We did lose several games in overtimes and last minute collapses due to fatigue. I liked to give each girl some rest during the game, but on occasions I would have to keep Omdahl and Wickstrom in for the entire 40 minutes. The big problem we faced was foul situations. At one time against Mesabi we finished the game with three players and on a few occasions would end up with four players.

Char finished the year with a 16.9 point scoring average while Julie and Gina were a shade under 10 points per game. We weren't exceptionally big but Lisa Caldwell and Gina Quirk did yeoman work on the rebounding side of the game. Each of these young lady athletes had their strong points and our chemistry on the team was super. This made our coaching job so much easier and we did not have to iron out any controversies or player problems. Omdahl, Wickstrom and Dicklich were good shooters, with Char and Michel excelling from the 3-point line. Julie was more of a driver and as a result got to shoot a lot of free throws. Quirk and Caldwell could rebound with most opposition and led the club in that department.

Becky Koslowski was the hustler, throwing her body all over the floor, but was prone to pick up fouls. A very sad footnote to our season was the untimely death of Becky as she was the victim of a traffic accident. I really miss her. She, on occasion, made my coaching life an adventure. I didn't know what she would do during the game and in most cases her actions usually helped our cause. But I would hold my breath when she made her daring dashes after a loose ball and collide with anything in her way.

The question of how to hold practices faced Tammy and me, and also how would we schedule them? With no more than seven players at any one time, I asked several male athletes (non-basketball players) to help us out by providing opposition for our drills and game situations practice. I believe this move helped our girls and I appreciated the time and effort the men provided. They were careful not to use strength and quickness to overpower our girls, thereby avoiding unnecessary injuries.

I can only remember one time when one of our girls got a little upset with me. In our third game of the year on the road down at Normandale, Michel questioned Tammy at half-time about why she was not getting playing time. Tammy transferred this question to me and I felt this was my fault and I had overlooked Michel in that first half. I

Fifty-Five Years on the Bench

changed that behavior real quick and my little Northwestern star responded by contributing full time to the operation of our games. I apologized to her for my error and told her we coaches were human and can make mistakes.

Although our season record was 5-15, I deemed the entire year a coaching success. The girls always played hard and they responded to our coaching philosophy 100%. Char set a women's basketball record over at Itasca when she converted seven 3-poiint field goals and ended up with 34 points. Gina and Lisa had big nights of their own with some terrific rebounding totals. Gina captured 21 boards against Brainerd in an overtime loss while Lisa pulled down 23 rebounds in a win over Itasca. The physical play from Becky resulted in a host of fouls as she averaged 4.3 fouls per game. But I would not react negatively to her hustle and drive. Anyway, some of those fouls were questionable!!

The type of game that hurt our team more than any other was a "walk up the floor" club that played basically a half court slow down game. Our kids liked to run, and when we were faced with a slow-down game we sometimes got impatient and forced action which resulted in physical mistakes. An example of our game problems came against Gogebic and Vermilion, both of whom slowed the game down and whipped us by 30 point spreads. So we lived with our running game and 3-point shooting, even though we had to do it with six players.

I was very sorry to see the season come to a close and disappointed that I couldn't get my girls to the State Tournament. I looked forward to each practice, all the games, and even the bus ride. Speaking of bus trips, I remember (through Char) how she and Julie were late for an out-of-town game bus ride. They had to fix macs & cheese and found they lacked milk to mix the ingredients. They solved the problem by adding more butter to make it melt and then wolfed it down just in time to catch the bus. According to Char's description, "We sit down to eat our wonderful concoction and we take a bite and we about gag – it was awful!" What a pair! They both served as Maids of Honor at their respective weddings. How's that for chemistry?

Richard W. Varichak

The lone negative experience concerning the program came after the season was over. The team asked me to come back as their coach for the next year. I was honored and proud to be asked to be their coach again and agreed to the request. I would be retired from the teaching profession but I thought it would be fun and fulfilling to associate myself with these super kids again. When I brought this request to the college president, he informed me that I would have to go through the normal procedure of applying for the position. This was surprising to say the least – I was their coach last year. I had 29 years of coaching experience, and now I had to prove that I was capable of coaching our women's basketball team! On the interview committee, in addition to the Women's Athletic Director, were two of the female faculty members, both of whom had been former students of mine. One was a coaching colleague of mine serving in the same department for the past 12 years. I thought the questions asked were a little ludicrous since they all knew me quite well. A week later, the president came into my classroom and informed me that the committee had selected a high school coach to lead the 1992-93 team. I was stunned with the decision and the president informed me that the committee members felt that the team needed a female role model as their coach. The girls were upset as they thought my rehiring as their coach would be a "slam dunk." Actually, so did I – so the decision was a little humiliating for me and disappointing that my female coaching colleagues decided to "dump" me. For Doug Schmitz, the men's basketball coach, this was his chance to acquire me as his assistant. For the next 16 years I then had the happy and exciting adventure working with the men's team and later with our Hibbing High School girls. Of that nice college team, only one sophomore came back the following year and the five recruits that I had persuaded to play for me did not come to Hibbing.

This one negative incident still did not dim the enjoyable season with these great six student athletes. I still keep in touch with them and have enjoyed a couple of reunions with some of them. I sincerely hope they will believe what an impact they had in my coaching life. Thanks girls!

Fifty-Five Years on the Bench

Tammy proved to be a very capable co-coach and quickly gained the respect of the team. I had no problem in sharing decisions concerning player evaluation along with team offense and defense. Our girls were all freshmen, so one big part of our job was to get them ready for college competition. She also was a valuable liaison between me and the girls which made for excellent team communication. I was hoping she would continue coaching but she had valid reasons not to and I respect her decision. Thanks Tammy!

Figure 62: Photo by Carol Lind – HCC Asst. Coach Tammy Varichak and Head Coach Dick Varichak

Figure 61: Photo by Carol Lind – HCC Head Coach Grandpa Varichak with Ball Girl Shawna Varichak

Chapter 18: Basketball Summer Camps - Are They Worth It?

When I look back on my athletic experiences, I feel I was born too early. I never had the luxury of being filmed during my games or had a chance to enjoy summer athletic camps. Most of our development came from individual practice or competitive action in our various recreational programs. In Chisholm, we were fortunate to have a dedicated recreational director named Guido "Swede" Pergol. Swede who was like a second father to us and under his influence and guidance Chisholm athletics prospered and bloomed.

In addition to the organized recreational activities offered by Swede and the city, most of us got together in free play and competition. I can remember during the summer months getting up early in the day, visiting my friends' homes and recruiting as many as we could wake up to play baseball, basketball, kick the can and numerous other games throughout the day. Little organization, lots of fun and we learned the essence of team play.

My first introduction to a summer basketball camp came in 1980 when I took my son, Don, to the University of North Dakota. Dave Gunther, the head basketball coach at NDU ran a big, very popular camp for both boys and girls. Mesabi Community College basketball coach Bill Wirtanen and I went out together with our two sons and we served as staff members of the camp. I was duly impressed with the organization and how the camp functioned. The campers were lodged in the college dormitories and the meals provided were plentiful and healthy. Coach Gunther introduced himself to the campers on the first day and was in attendance all five days, helping with the drills and motivating both campers and staff members. He assigned the staff members to drills which accentuated their strong coaching points. Since I had some offensive strengths, I received shooting and fast break drills.

Fifty-Five Years on the Bench

The campers were divided into groups for instruction and drills. There was a senior group consisting of grades 10-12 and a junior division of 7th – 9th graders. Although Don was in the junior group, he was chosen as a starting guard in the 10th-12th grade All-Star game on the last day of the camp. He had a good camp and I could see he was going to be an asset to the Hibbing Bluejacket cage squad in the near future. His team won the game and he contributed seven points from his point guard position.

The following year, I took both Don and my daughter Pam to the camp. Don did his consistent good work and was chosen to play in the All-Star game again. But it was Pam who stole the show in the girls' 7th-9th group. She won 5 of the 6 competitions but strangely was not chosen as the most outstanding camper. It was explained to me that they wanted to pass the awards "around." The head coach for the Lakehead University girls' team from Thunder Bay, Canada, came up to me and said he wanted to give Pam a basketball scholarship (she was only in 7th grade). He said he would hold it until she graduated from high school.

After those two years of Gunther –led camps, I came to the conclusion that he ran one of the best camps in the country. I was fortunate to work in a few other camps but some fell below what I considered worthwhile. One camp I visited (my grand-daughters were enrolled) featured both boys and girls. Since I had the two grand-daughters in the camp, I stuck around and watched the proceedings all week. I found that the drills did not start on time, they were loosely run and the boys received much more attention from the staff. The head of the camp made his initial appearance on the first day and then did not show up the rest of the week. Staff members, prior to the start of the day's action, were shooting baskets, dunking the ball and hogging the basketballs while campers sat around doing nothing. What a waste of time (and money)!

My involvement with local summer camps began with a staff assignment with the Dick Larson Bluejacket camp at Hibbing High School. The popular Jacket coach brought both me and Doug Schmitz aboard and his camp proved to be a motivating experience for me and the campers. The camp was only for boys and gave me a chance to work

Richard W. Varichak

with the first of many grandchildren, Beau Jacobson. Dick used a combination of his varsity players to work with the younger players while utilizing adult coaches to lead the older campers. I found his camp very organized and educational and used many of his ideas when Doug and I started our own camps.

Doug and I started our own camp experience when he got the head boys basketball post at Nashwauk-Keewatin in 1997. Two more of my grandchildren were participants in the younger division. Travis Varichak, son of my daughter, Pam, and Kyle Jacobson, youngest child of my daughter, Vikki, proved to be outstanding campers. Both were part of my 5-on-5 team and dominated the opposition in our daily games. I thought at this time they both would be assets to their respective high school basketball teams. Neither one ended up on the court – Travis is now pursuing a welding education at Mesabi Community College while

Figure 63: Photo by Tom Lindstrom
Nashwauk-Keewatin Boys Basketball Camp 1997
Instructors: Dick Varichak, Doug Schmitz, Dick Larson, Todd Hoenstein

Fifty-Five Years on the Bench

Kyle, after playing football and wrestling for the Hibbing Bluejackets, is at Itasca Community College to get a degree in Natural Sciences and wrestled for the Vikings.

After a three year stay at Nashwauk-Keewatin, the Schmitz-Varichak combination moved over to Bluejacket land and the girls' program. The program was in a spiral downward and we thought a girls' camp would help to regenerate the interest the girls seem to have lost.

The camp would be of special interest to me because I had some grand-daughters who would be participating. Shawna Varichak and Lindsay Jacobson went on to play at the varsity level while Taylor Varichak ended her basketball participation in 9th grade to concentrate on Volleyball. Vanessa Jacobson traded in her tenner shoes to join the cheerleading units serving both hockey and wrestling.

Figure 64: Photo by Larry Ryan
Run & Shoot Girls' 2004 Basketball Camp Instructors
Brittany Herzog, Breanna Herzog, Dave Hillman, Dick Varichak, Dani O'Bannion, Doug Schmitz, Julie Schmitz, Jeff Buffetta, Erica Lister.

Our first camp drew 48 campers, which we felt was a good start. We were fortunate to get some top-notch staff members such as Jim Kne from the Bluestreaks, Jeff Buffetta and his brother, Brian Buffetta from Mt. Iron-Buhl, and Dave Hillman from Mesabi East. Kurt Zeidmulder

Richard W. Varichak

from Hibbing Community College, my brother, George Varichak, Don Stahl, former HCC star and Greg Helstrom, current Bluejacket coach also were instrumental in running the camp. We also persuaded strong instructors such as Susan Roy, Kaye Anderson, Anne Swanson and husband, Rick Swanson to join our forces. We utilized some of our past campers to work with the younger kids and this move worked to perfection. The young ones idolized their instructors and demonstrated their affection with a lot of hugs and hand holding. At times, we could spot some future teachers who impressed us with their teaching methods.

One of the rewards which came out of our summer camp was the opportunity to work with and get to know campers who represented some of our opposing schools. Jenna Beckner came in from Bigfork where she paced her high school team to winning seasons in her varsity years. She culminated her basketball career by leading Bigfork to State tournament competition in her senior year. We had three delightful girls from Eveleth-Gilbert. Rachel Perushek, Krista Perushek, and their sister McKenzie Perushek participated for several years and Rachel returned as one of our staff members. We had to twist McKenzie's arm to come in as a camper, but once she joined, she proved to be highly competitive. Rachel and Krista both went on to Mesabi Community College and Rachel transferred to St. Scholastica to play softball. She finished her two years at Mesabi, participating in both volleyball and basketball. Kristina Lindfors, a Virginia cager, enjoyed our camp for three years and came back to demonstrate her basketball education when our Bluejackets faced Virginia during the

Figure 65: Photo by Don Peterson
Hibbing High School Run & Shoot
2008 Basketball Camp
Krista & Rachel Perusheck from the Eveleth-Gilbert team in their third year at the camp.

Fifty-Five Years on the Bench

season. There was always good-natured kidding between the visiting players and our coaching staff, even to the hug or two before the game started. Elizabeth Sletten and Leah Fillman honored us with their presence at our camp and both girls were instrumental in leading Nashwauk-Keewatin to state playoffs. Kacey Kusistto from Greenway, along with Risa Valentini and Alyssa Amic from Chisholm gave us some more Iron Range Conference mix.

We were very pleased with the turnout from our own girls' team. Usually all the varsity girls were in attendance and our total numbers jumped to 92 campers in our last year that Doug and I ran the camp. Our basic philosophy in setting the camp up was to give all campers a chance to enhance their skills and understanding of the game of basketball. It was not set up to be a financial success and in most cases we did not have a money making venture. On occasion, we invited a girl or two, who could not afford the camp fee, to join us anyway. We felt the goodwill brought about by this action was more important than refusing the applicant.

Figure 66: Photo by Larry Ryan
Bluejacket 2004 Run & Shoot Basketball Camp

The camper who came from the furthest distance to enjoy our instruction was Andrea Harmon from Portland, Oregon. Of course, our camp was not nationally known, but her grandfather, George Varichak, was one of our instructors and both were spending a few weeks with

Richard W. Varichak

Noka and me. Andrea was a pretty good athlete and did well at the camp, but ended up playing high school and college soccer.

I strongly believe that summer basketball camps are worth the time and effort. Although there are some team competition phases in each camp, the important part of the instruction is in the evaluation process, of not only our camp, but sister camps through the State of Minnesota; high points were awarded on the learning and retention of fundamentals learning.

Figure 67: Photo by Larry Ryan
Basketball Buddies Program
The beginning of the Bluejackets Basketball Program – 113 future cage stars – 2008
Grades K-6th

Chapter 19: Parents Can Be Fun

When young aspiring coaches choose to enter the coaching profession, one of the relationships they seem to overlook is the parental contribution to their education. As coaches become involved with their athletes, the family becomes more important as involvement increases. This is very evident on the elementary, middle, and high school levels. Parental pressure seems to evaporate on the two-year and four-year college experience.

For example – in my first year of coaching public school competition, I was faced with an irate father of one of my high school basketball players. He wanted to punch me in the nose because I did not play his son in a playoff game. And this was in my first year of coaching! On the other hand, I served as a coach for 29 years at Hibbing Community College and received only one telephone call regarding a player. That player was my brother who I had to take out of the game periodically because of a heart condition. The telephone caller wanted to know why I was pulling my brother out of the game so often. That call was the lone question concerning my tenure in college coaching.

I found a comfort level in my task as an assistant coach, especially in my experience with middle school and high school girl athletes. Working with Doug Schmitz proved to be some of the most enjoyable years of coaching. As the head coach, Doug took any heat which developed among certain parents. I was fortunate to escape the "heat" in most cases and at times had to soothe some of the hurt feelings when Doug had to point out physical and mental miscues. Doug sometimes referred to our relationship as "good cop – bad cop" but I don't think he really believed it. I know I probably had players mad at me when a situation came up in which I had to "crack the whip." I can remember shouting out to my grand-daughter, "Lindsay Mae! Get off the floor," as I reminded her to jump higher on rebounding. I don't think she was especially happy with me at those moments. I was aware, also, that two girls quit

Fifty-Five Years on the Bench

the squad because they thought Coach Varichak was too tough and expected too much of the players. One of them commented, "Coach Schmitz would be better off without Varichak." So, although I basically enjoyed the relationship with most of my players, there were a few who did not accept me 100% as their coach. Strange as it seems, the parents of the two players did not confront me concerning their action. I don't think the parents actually cared one way or another.

During the many years I served as a coach, I was introduced to a variety of parental relationships. These experiences for the most part were positive and fulfilling. In each of my movements from high school to college and back to high school coaching, I would rate parent cooperation and behavior almost 100% in my relationship with moms and dads.

There were a number of parents who impressed me with their attitudes, how they dealt with the coaches and their contribution to athletic programs, and how they directed their offspring to positive outlets. I discovered our first parental support in my opening teaching and coaching job in Evant, Texas. This was a small Class B school in central Texas and farming was the basic occupation of most residents. I enjoyed the two years at Evant and the relationship with special parents. Buddy and Lenore Arnold came forward early and made us feel right at home. Their daughter, Carolyn Arnold, was my outstanding basketball player and valedictorian of her graduation class. These two fine people are still close friends with Noka and me, as well as Carolyn, who we have kept close to our hearts.

Figure 68: Photo by Carolyn Arnold
Buddy & Lenore Arnold
Evant, Texas 1960-62
Parents of Carolyn – Basketball

Richard W. Varichak

Another super set of parents, Curtis and Catherine Koerth, made sure that their two children were students first and athletes second. Their son, Ervin, a senior, was an all-around stud, starring in both football and basketball. Daughter, Rosalyn was a sophomore starter on my basketball team and was very instrumental in our District Championship. I can still remember Curtis giving me some direct orders. "If Ervin and Rosalyn ever give you any guff, let me know and I will tan their hides!" Fortunately, both kids were excellent individuals and never gave me any grief.

As we left Evant to head up north to the Texas panhandle and my next assignment in Darrouzett, I wondered what kind of experiences I would face in this small Class B school. I now assumed extra responsibilities as the high school principal, in addition to my teaching load and girls' basketball coach. One of the smart moves we made was to rent a farmhouse three miles out of town without a telephone. I figured I would have enough situations to handle as a coach and principal. The year went by without too much controversy, but I did have to suspend one of my basketball players from school for 3 days because of a stupid action on her part after a tourney game. When I informed the school board, I got backing from the Board President who fully agreed with my action. This was important to me because the Board President was the father of the suspended girl. The mother was not in agreement though and made a trip out to my house to tearfully beg me to change my decision. The daughter's suspension cost her the class valedictorian honor but I could not change my mind.

Three other sets of parents made my professional experience a positive one in Darrouzett that year. The Harry Jergenson family became close friends, although I was not the coach for their children. Their oldest son, Scotty, was an all-around standout performing on the football, basketball and baseball teams. The parents' interest in education was highly reflected in the academic success of their offspring. Faye and George Schoenhals became fast friends although I was not involved as the coach for their sons, who were good athletes and performers in the classroom. We still keep in touch with both George and Faye to this day,

Fifty-Five Years on the Bench

although our correspondence is usually centered on the trading of Christmas cards.

As I progressed up the educational ladder and my hiring at Hibbing Community College in 1963, parent confrontation became almost nil. There were moms and dads at games and parent attendance at our end of the year athletic banquets. But as I mentioned previously, I received only one telephone call in 29 years of coaching at the college and that call wasn't even from a player's parent.

Two negative incidents involving our players' families do come to mind, both varsity basketball players. One of my freshman cagers had some problems with his dad who had taken to drinking heavily since his wife had passed away. He attended our home games in an inebriated state most of the times and was quite vocal in the criticism of his son's play. I finally had enough during one game and asked him to leave the gym. He was belligerent and at first did not obey my request. Finally, after I threatened to call a police officer, he relented and left. He later apologized and did not repeat his verbal abuse of his son.

The other incident involved one of our women basketball players. Actually, the complaining adult was the uncle of the player who had come from California. He was upset with a situation in which he believed his niece and the coaching staff was having some difficulties. His tirade was aimed at me as Athletic Director and the fact that he and I had been football teammates at the college. After speaking to both the coaching staff and his niece, the problem was resolved to everyone's satisfaction.

I enjoyed a few parental relationships at Hibbing Community College because of their strong interest and cooperation in our athletic programs. Bill and Rita Loushine were strong backers of our teams while their son, Bob, became one of our outstanding basketball players. Bob and Shari Schlagel from Rush City attended most of our games to follow their son, Cory, our sharp-shooting point guard. They would travel all the way to Ely on a Wednesday night to watch our Hibbing – Vermilion clash, a distance of about 325 miles round trip. That's parental support! Both Bill Loushine and Bob Schlagel were part of my athletic life, one as a coach and one as a player. Loushine was my high school baseball coach

Richard W. Varichak

and we celebrated a state baseball championship together. As the Hibbing Community College basketball coach, I tried to persuade Schlagel to come and play for me, but lost him to St. Cloud State University. Well, things finally worked out as we got this son twenty years later.

The Schmitz-Varichak coaching duo moved over several miles to Nashwauk when Doug took over as boys' basketball boss for the N-K Spartans. We both knew that Nashwauk-Keewatin teams could be very athletic and the parents could be tough on coaches. In our three year tenure with the Spartans, Doug turned the boys' program around without too much parent confrontation. Bill Salmi was one of our biggest supporters and his son, Tom, proved to be one of our most productive players. Bill made the statement one evening at one of our home games, "I look at our bench and I see three coaches (Schmitz, Varichak, Dick Larson) sitting there with 100 years of experience, so I know enough to keep my mouth shut." Yet one father who had two sons playing complained heavily about the lack of playing time involving the senior boy. Actually the sophomore brother was a much better ball player and received most of the floor time.

Although Doug improved the N-K boys' basketball program to the tune of 51 wins and 25 losses, he was let go after three years. He was told it was a numbers decision but he believed the administration bowed to the pressure of a few parents. This move proved to be the Spartans loss and Hibbing girls' basketball program's gain.

Our next coaching stop was back in Hibbing again as we took over the Bluejacket girls basketball squads. After a one year stint at Mora High School, Doug joined me as the seventh grade girls coach. This was the start of great parent support right through until we gave up the reins nine years later.

The girls' basketball Hoop Club has been a vital cog in maintaining a high level of team competition through their financial support. The school district does cover expenses incurred with officiating and transportation, but supplies such as uniforms, basketballs, banquet awards and the hiring of charter busses for long trips comes out of the Hoop Club budget. The makeup of the club basically included the parents of the

Fifty-Five Years on the Bench

basketball players, but the coaches were also included for their input on how to spend the funds which were raised during the year. The coaches were extremely pleased with the basic orders from the club, "Spend the money!" The coaching staff did as ordered because we were never denied our many requests. Through the Hoop Club, Doug and I developed some great relationships with many of the parents. But of course, it was not all "hearts and roses" as we faced a couple of dissatisfied players and parents in our eight-year tenure. I know of two players who decided not to continue their basketball participation because "Varichak is not a good coach" or "Varichak expects too much from the players." Also, Doug had his share of parent dissent, but on the whole, both of us received unquestioned support from the majority of the moms and dads.

Figure 69: Photo from Terri Miesbauer
Bob & Kathy Nyberg - parents of Nicole, Melissa, & Christine (2001-2011)
Terri & Mike Miesbauer – parents of Hannah, Rebekah, & Rachel (2001-2011)

Many of our parent-coach relationships began in our 7th grade "fab nine" group. The players racked up a 60-10 record in the two years we had them and the relationship became very close. As a result, we had a group of young ladies who were not only talented but very cerebral and

Richard W. Varichak

this made the coaching experience a highly positive one. Bob and Kathy Nyberg came into the picture early as they sent three daughters through our program. Both were natural leaders and Kathy served as one of the strongest presidents of the Hoop Club. Bob served the program in various duties and reminded me of his dad, who I had the pleasure of helping coach our Little League baseball team 34 years ago. Mike and Terri Miesbauer, both educators, also saw three of their daughters play for the Jackets. Their eldest, Hannah, gave us the most laughable moment when we asked her if she was a left or right handed. She didn't know as a 7th grader and although we found out she was a natural southpaw, she learned to shoot with either hand. All three girls were solid contributors to our program, although they did not break into the starting lineup. This didn't seem to bother their parents, an attitude that you don't see very often. What a positive twosome!

Figure 70 Photo from Sandy Ongaro
Sandy Ongaro – parent of Nikki Klinck (2001-2007)

Sandy Ongaro and the Burdicks, Linda and Randy, were always in attendance at games and would give us a hug and handshake, win or lose, after the contest. Sandy's daughter, Nikki, and the Burdick girls, Stacy and Michelle, were vital cogs in the Bluejackets race to conference and section championships.

I couldn't forget our two coaches, whose daughters were so valuable in our fab nine years and later on as varsity regulars. Head Coach

Figure 71: Photo by Larry Ryan
Doug & Kathy Schmitz – parents of Jodi Schmitz (2001- 2007)

Fifty-Five Years on the Bench

Doug Schmitz and wife Kathy, along with youngest daughter, Jodi, were part of my life since 1972 when Doug played for me. Jodi was the pepper-pot point guard no bigger than a minute, but was a giant on the court with her shooting and ball handling. At times I felt her dad was a little too tough with her and that's where I came in, to soothe some hurt feelings and to admonish her father at times. But Jodi knew she was loved by her parents and could always come to her other "Grandpa Dick" when she needed him.

Jeff Jacobson served as our volunteer coach for the varsity and his wife, Vikki (my beautiful daughter), were avid supporters of their daughter, Lindsay, as she progressed from one of the "fab nine" to a valuable contributor to Jacket fortunes. Of course, Lindsay Mae, along with her two loving parents, contributed highly to my love for coaching.

Figure 72: Picture by Tom Lindstrom
Vikki & Jeff Jacobson – parents of Lindsay Jacobson (2001-2007)

It was ironic that one of my parental conflicts was with my own head coach. Doug and I had periodic disagreements but nothing that could not be ironed out quickly. But this problem involved my granddaughter Lindsay, in her senior year of competition. After being a part of the starting unit early in the year, Doug decided to have her come off the bench as part of the second unit. This was a blow to Lindsay who was visibly upset with the decision. I did not agree with Doug and we had a couple of heated discussions concerning the move. This put me in a tight spot because of my position on the team, but I readily explained to Doug that my recommendation to reinstate Lindsay to a starter was a player evaluation, not a grandfather's request. Statistically, Lindsay led the team in numerous categories. Doug stuck to his decision and did not make the change, but I felt this was one error in judgment on his part. I will say he

Richard W. Varichak

didn't make many mistakes in evaluating players, but we are all human! Lindsay went on to a successful college basketball career, leading her team to participation in two state tournaments.

Rick and Regina Brant gave us Amber, our bean-pole low post center. Skinny as a rail, Amber held her own on under-the-hoop conflicts and rebounded well for her lack of girth. Both Brants were exceptionally warm to us and were faithful followers of the team from 7th to 12th grade.

Figure 73: Photo by Larry Ryan Linda & Bill Manney – parents of Kelly (2001-2007)

Kelly Manney, one of our fab nine players, rarely experienced being a starter but proved to be a valuable reserve off the bench. Bill and Linda Manney never complained about Kelly's situation and seemed to be very happy that she contributed to a good program. I marveled at Bill's restraints at games – he never seemed too get upset or excited.

The Graheks, John and Marcia, along with the McLaughlins, Paul and Kim, usually went out of their way to help the coaching staff. Both families put on team get-togethers and Marcia was instrumental in many team functions. Kim proved to be an accurate statistician and both wives continually refused my money during my quests for coffee at the concession stand. On cold winter nights after the game, I did not look forward to going outside to scrape my car windows. But lo and behold – on several occasions I found Paul or John busily scraping the windows, thus saving me from a cold, miserable task. Incidentally, Paul was the dad who suggested that I write a book, after listening to my many tales covering my coaching life.

Figure 74: Photo from McLaughlins Paul & Kim McLaughlin parents of Katie (2008-2011)

Fifty-Five Years on the Bench

Peg and Dr. Dan Lister were instrumental in the progress of our girls' program. Peg gave much of her time to the basketball Hoop Club while she and Dan made sure they were at each game, supporting their daughters Erica and Diana.

I also found my son Don a cooperative and caring parent in his relation with the coaching staff. I was happy to be able to coach his oldest daughter, Shawna, on my Washington 6th grade team, also on her 8th grade team, and two years with the varsity. His younger daughter, Taylor, was my fourth grade star and varsity performer. Don was instrumental in giving his daughters individual attention as far as basketball skills were involved and since he played for Doug in college his teaching techniques were comparable to our basketball philosophy.

Figure 75: Photo by Ann Staniger Don Varichak parent of Shawna, Taylor, and Cole

Executive Sports Writer Rick Weegman of the Duluth News Tribune investigated, through a series of articles in 2002, the relationship and influences of parents on coaches' lives.[2] He cited several coaches who blamed parents for the loss of their jobs and some who quit the coaching profession because of the turmoil. Be he did report several positive remarks by coaches in an article entitled "Problem Parents are in the Minority."

"Obviously not all parents are to blame. The vast majority don't cause trouble. "Ninety-nine percent of the parents in our school district are very supportive," [Randy] Myhre said.

In 25 years as a football, hockey and baseball coach, Silver Bay's Doug Conboy never heard any gripes. "In all that time, I had four calls from parents and they all were for the same thing: they wanted to know if I needed help shoveling the snow off the field," said Conboy, now principal at Cook County High School in Grand Marais.

Richard W. Varichak

The same applied to [Rod] Eidelbes, who left Grand Rapids after 14 years at the helm. He stepped down after guiding the Thunderhawks to a third-place finish in the Class AAA state tournament in March, leaving the team to assistant Dan Elhard. "Overall, for me there was a lot of support from parents," Eidelbes said. "That was one of the more enjoyable features of coaching."

But coaching had become a year-round job for Eidelbes. Camps and tournaments took up much of his time in the summer. "That's one of the things you might not consider when you start out," said Eidelbes, referring to a Minnesota State High School League rule change that allows coaches to coach their athletes during the summer. "How, to be competitive, you're compelled to do that."

John and Chris Matetich contributed their three daughters to our program under our watch. Anna, the eldest of the three, turned out to be one of our most prolific performers and went on to star at Concordia College in Moorhead, Minnesota. Misa carried on the Matetich tradition, captained the Blue Jacket squad, played at Itasca Community College, and finished her collegiate career at Crown College in St. Bonifacious, Minnesota. Tina, the youngest, is still playing for the Blue Jackets. Chris was a regular contributor in Hoop Club events and held team dinners in their home. John also took time off from his business to help coach our middle school teams.

Tom and Sue Jamar, parents of Erin, were two of the hardest working parents in our program. Very active in Hoop Club activities, they made me feel more important than I perceived myself. Sue always made sure my coffee on game nights was "on the house." It's nice to know you are appreciated!

I came across an informative guide for coaches and how they can start to establish a meaningful relationship with parents, from the Minnesota State High School Bulletin, released in September, 2009.[3] Doug and I both noted that our program followed this guide quite closely and I believe that's a big factor in our teams' success. The six basic points are outlined in the following presentation.

Fifty-Five Years on the Bench

Point 1: Emergency Procedures: Have a clear plan about how an emergency will be handled. Have the parents provide the information necessary for you to handle an emergency (parents' names, addresses, telephone numbers, names and telephone numbers of family doctors and the hospital of preference). You should also describe the procedures that will be used in case of an emergency.

Point 2: Understanding the Sport: Many times during the course of the season, spectators question officials, shout instructions to players or contradict the coach because they are unaware of the rules or lack a basic understanding of the sport. This can often place a strain on the coach/parent relationship. By reviewing some basic concepts and rules, you can help avoid these situations. Explain what equipment the players need and where it can be purchased. You may also want to offer advice on the quality of equipment, and indicate how much parents can expect to pay for specific items.

Point 3: Parents' Responsibilities: Create awareness of ethics and sportsmanship and how they relate to sports and activities. Explain to the parents that their child is counting on them to be a positive participant at their event. The main reason kids play is to have fun and be with their friends. Give participants a scenario of attending and observing a math class at the school. While sitting in the back of the room, begin to act out and yell at the teacher. Continue to act poorly while shouting "That teach never calls on my kid, he/she must hate my kid, they never give her a chance…" Conclude by asking the parents, "Would you act like this in a math class?" Then remind the parents that high school athletics venues are also classrooms, just a different subject matter and that it is not OK to yell and scream at the players, coaches or officials. The Team Up binder sent to schools this past fall has a terrific resource: "TeamUp for Sportsmanship," an educational DVD video, as well as a parent's handbook. Next school year Team Up will include the "TeamUp for Sportsmanship – Officials Perspective" educational video.

Point 4: Communication Expectations: Promote the importance of ongoing, honest communication. Playing time, strategy, play calling and another student participant are not appropriate items for a parent to discuss with their child's coach. Explain your school's communication protocol. There are situations that may require a conference between the coach and the parent. These are to be encouraged. It is important that both parties involved have a clear understanding of the other's position. When these conferences are necessary, the following procedure should be followed to help promote a resolution to the issue of concern. Call to set up an appointment. If the coach cannot be reached, call the athletics/activities director. He or she will help facilitate. Do not attempt to confront a coach before or after a contest or practice. These can be emotional times for both the parent and the coach. Meetings of this nature do not promote resolution.

Point 5: Season Schedule: Provide the student participants and their parents with a schedule of games and practices for the upcoming season. Also, inform the parents as to when players are expected to arrive at practices and games and when they will be available to leave. You may also wish to provide a list of all the players' addresses and phone numbers for the parents.

Point 6: Question and Answer Time: Concluding the meeting with a question-and-answer period will provide parents with an opportunity to raise any concerns they may have.

Parents can be a great asset for your program. By offering a pre-season meeting and setting clear expectations, you are setting the groundwork needed for a great season.

When I look back on all my experiences with the various parents in my coaching tenure, I have to mention my most favorite pair. Their names are George and Mae Varichak, who happen to be the two who raised me. They made sure I had the opportunity to participate in as many activities as were offered to me. When I was in high school, I mentioned to my Dad that maybe I should find a job and help the family income. My father's remark was, "Son, you have all your life to work at a job, but only one chance to play high school athletics. Finish your sports participation and then go find a job." So I started out my parental relationships on the highest note of my athletic and professional endeavors.

Fifty-Five Years on the Bench

Figure 76: Photo by Arnie Maki
The most important set of parents who made my life and profession a memorable and fulfilling experience are my own. Thank you George and Mae Varichak.

Chapter 20: Student Team Managers Run the Show

In many of my coaching experiences, especially on the college level, I have maintained I recruit team managers first, and then I go after the players. As a coach, we are faced with many decisions concerning player evaluation, x's and o's, scouting, scheduling and many other duties which lead to running a successful program. But there exist a number of mundane duties which a coach would have a difficult time to fit in his/her busy schedule. This is where that indispensible manager comes into the picture.

On the high school level, you usually get a volunteer who wants to be with the team because their friends are the athletes who make up the squad. You may get students anywhere from the freshman grade up to a senior. With this younger group there will be much teaching and sometimes a lack of responsibility. I found the situation a little better with the college programs. I enjoyed managers who were ex-servicemen, ex-high school managers and who were, on the whole, more mature and responsible.

I was blessed in my first year at Evant High School when I inherited three top-notch managers. My football manager for two years was Waylan Munday. He came to see me on my first day in Evant and asked for the manager's job. A sophomore, he looked a little frail and I was worried about his ability to move some of our heavy equipment around. But my fears were allayed when I observed his workhorse work ethic. He usually was waiting for me as we prepared for practice and was always asking me if I had any more duties for him. He was a whiz on remembering the players' uniform numbers and made sure our game programs were correct. Waylan began in a long list of superb team managers who made my coaching tenure a pleasant and enjoyable experience.

As I moved into the basketball season, I was once again fortunate to get a top-notch manager in the person of Kay Belvin for my girls' cage

Fifty-Five Years on the Bench

team. Kay was a senior, highly intelligent, and her work ethic was terrific. Kay was a quiet individual, sort of shy, so her experience with the superintendent of schools gave us a big laugh. It seems that Kay had to go into the men's locker room to get some equipment. Upon entering the room, she discovered Mr. Greer, our super, using the facilities. Both of them made a quick exit from the locker room, highly embarrassed. Poor Kay had a difficult time in facing Greer the next few days and kept away from him as much as possible. Although Kay was not a high school varsity athlete, she has made a name for herself in the bowling world.

Figure 77: Photo by A.E. Greer
Kay Belvin – Basketball Manager
Evant H.S. - 1961

My tiger-tough football center, Eldon Perkins, became my boys' basketball manager, much to my delight. Eldon was a stickler for detail and I never had to worry about uniforms, scorebook, road game schedules, etc. That kid saved me a lot of minutes and gave me time to teach and coach basketball. I always called him "Perk" for short and this led to an amusing incident, involving Perkins, my wife, Noka, and our brand new 6-week old puppy. The young dog was given to us as a gift – his mother had milk fever so she was unable to feed him. We solved that dilemma by taking my daughter's doll baby bottle and thus Perky, our puppy, could get his fill of milk. But back to the incident. Perky had done something Noka didn't like about

Figure 78: Photo by A.E. Greer
Eldon Perkins & Assistant Melinda Mittel – Basketball Managers
Evant H.S. 1961

Richard W. Varichak

the time that Eldon was about to knock on our door to ask me something concerning the team. Noka shouted, "PERK, GET OUT OF THERE!" And our poor manager, hearing his name from an irate wife, wheeled around and started to make a hasty retreat from our door. Noka had to run after him and convince him that she was talking to our puppy and not to him. Eldon has remained in Evant and is one of the best barbeque cooks in the state of Texas.

In 1963, I moved my family to Hibbing, Minnesota to undertake the education of student athlete who matriculates at Hibbing Junior College. One of my athletic assignments was the men's basketball team. As I gathered my candidates for the team, I was pleased to see Jon Timpane among the bodies assembled as he was recommended to me by Elmer Salvog, the Hibbing High School football coach. Elmer told me that Jon was the best manager he ever had and this proved to be accurate in my case as well. Jon, an ex-Air Force serviceman, brought organization, hard work and dedication to his position as team manager and I was fortunate to have him for three years.

Figure 79: Photo by Hibbing Daily Tribune
Jon Timpane – Basketball Manager
Hibbing Junior College 1964-66

Jon passed the baton of leadership to one of our outstanding football players. Mike Zakula, ex- Buhl Bulldog, finished his grid career at Hibbing as the 6th leading rusher in the nation as one of our halfbacks. Mike stood only at 5'8" but was one tough football giant and as a team basketball manager he made my job very pleasant for two years. He demanded cleanliness and order and the players were afraid to displease him. He kicked me off the basketball court one time because I had my street shoes on. He admonished me several times because he thought the

Fifty-Five Years on the Bench

locker room should be neater. Today, Dr. Mike Zakula is a highly respected orthodontist and has even serviced members of my family.

I received another plus in the managerial stable of good people when I lucked out and recruited All-American Frank Russ and teammates Kenny Lee, Tom Tintor, Bob Edelstein, and Merty Hirt from the Hibbing Bluejackets. I also obtained the services of Mr. Tom White. Tom displayed a strong commitment to the program and like Timpane and Zakula there was no fear in handing them your school keys. I also enjoyed years where we had no stolen equipment which amazed some of our faculty and administration. Tom went on to a teaching career, following Frank Russ to the Hermantown School district, where they both enjoyed a teaching and coaching career.

Figure 80: Photo by Hibbing Daily Tribune
Mike Zakula – Basketball Manager
Hibbing State Junior College - 1973

Some other team managers who made my life a little easier included Al Avelsgaard, another ex-serviceman, Eldon Kruchowski and Peder Gilbert. All three were go-getters although Avelsgaard wanted to be more of a coach than a manager. He eventually did go into the coaching field, leading both college and international squads.

Another tough football player from Buhl gave me a couple of good years. Frank Bigelow was the ball-swinging manager I mentioned in our episode in the Gogebic donney brook. When I was ejected from the game, Frank had to fight his

Figure 81: Photo by Dick Varichak
Al Avelsgard – Basketball Manager
Hibbing Junior College - 1979

Richard W. Varichak

way off the floor, swinging a bag of basketballs and sending a couple of Gogebic students home with a headache. Frank also gave me a huge fright in my swimming class. He attempted to swim underwater for too long a distance, lost consciousness and had to be pulled out of the water. He put some gray hair on my blonde locks that day.

Denny Rice – aah yes! He absolutely gave our program life, humor and nearly drove me crazy. Pint-sized Denny was an organizer, always giving me suggestions on what we could do to make the program better, richer, and how we should entice the best athletes to come to HSJC. But his crowning achievement was the meal arrangement he made in Moorhead at the end of a tiring three-day basketball trip through North Dakota and Western Minnesota. We had just defeated the Moorhead State J.V. that afternoon and I thought the team would like a sit-down meal in a swank restaurant. After getting the kids seated and ready to order, I sought the restaurant boss to make arrangements for payment. Upon my return to the section where we were located, I saw, much to my astonishment, bottles of champagne on each table. Mr. Rice had snookered the establishment to "donate" the bubbly (he actually incurred the cost). But there our team sat with liquor before them and wearing beautiful team blazers with Hibbing State Junior College emblazoned across their left chest. Needless to say, I was livid and quickly cleared the table before the kids could take part in Dennis Rice's plans. I also cursed the stupid politicians who had a voice in lowering the drinking age to eighteen. Dennis stayed away from me for the next few days, and I let him suffer for awhile. So much for college days!

When Doug and I moved over to the high school picture, we were once again very fortunate in obtaining the services of several outstanding managers. Aleesha Harris came to us in our first year and stayed with us for three years. What a fine young lady! If she wasn't sure what we wanted, she wasn't bashful about getting our instructions repeated to her satisfaction. Once you outlined the procedures for practice and game situations, she would follow these procedures religiously and if we made a switch on them, it never bothered her.

Fifty-Five Years on the Bench

Tom Keeler and Angela Norman served as both manager and video operators. I noticed a vast improvement in our game films during their tenure with the camera but they were just as effective on the court and equipment room. Angel Beckman tried her hand at making the team and played up to 9th grade. But her managerial skills were more proficient than her basketball skills. Having played the sport, she understood the needs and the demands of the players and coaching staff.

During our last two years with the Bluejacket girls we inherited a diminutive pepper-pot manager named Jess Gielen. No bigger than a minute, Jess reminded us of "Radar" on the sitcom "Mash." Doug was amazed that Jess could anticipate what he wanted before he mentioned it to her. I commented on watching her shoot a basketball that she had pretty good technique. Her answer to that was, "Hey, Coach! When I was in third grade, I started playing basketball. I happened to be on your grand-daughter's (Taylor) team. One day you came to our practice to teach us how to shoot. I will always remember what you told us. You said, 'If you shoot right, it doesn't matter if you make it or miss it, the ball will come back to you.' I thought about that every time I took a shot when I played and even remember it now."

Figure 82: Photo by Larry Ryan
Tom Keeler – Basketball Manager
Hibbing High School 2004-06

So to all you team managers who graced our coaching life, many thanks for making the job easier and more meaningful. I found a recurring theme in the character of these young men and women who reflected the traits of commitment, loyalty, and dedication. We now know who "runs the machine."

Chapter 21: The Last Hurrah!

As I look back over the past 55 years of my coaching career, I marvel at how fast those years have gone by. I basically got the coaching bug at a very young age, while I was competing in Junior High athletics. The idea of putting together a group of novices and developing them into a cohesive unit to win contests really appealed to me. The X's and O's were more important to me initially, not realizing that fundamentals were much more important in the early stages of teaching the sport.

When I finished the basketball season in 2008, I knew it was time to retire. How did I know? First of all, there was the daily commitment to be at practice each day at a designated time. Although I enjoyed the practices when I was there, it was the *thought* that I had to be somewhere each day. The bus rides (especially in those cramped school buses) were getting old and more uncomfortable each year. A big factor was the loss of grand-daughters on the team roster. Lindsay and Taylor were done in 2007 and I knew I would miss those beautiful faces when practice sessions opened up the next year.

On the other hand, I knew I would miss the company

Figure 83: Photo by Larry Ryan
Coach Varichak announces his retirement from the Bluejacket Girls Basketball program - 2008

of all our fine young ladies who made the job so pleasant. The thought of getting ready on game night, the game itself, and the close relationship with the coaching staff were factors that would be sorely missed.

Fifty-Five Years on the Bench

There were other fine people who helped make this coaching experience a fulfilling and enjoyable venture. I would be remiss if I didn't mention a group of school employees who were instrumental in helping my coaching efforts. The custodial staffs made it a little easier to carry out our duties. First, there was the father-son combo of Jeff and Dobbs Watson in Darrouzett, Texas. Dobbs was the son who couldn't do enough for me until his father, Jeff, admonished him one time, "don't you go and spoil that young coach," but said it with a twinkle in his eyes. What a pair!

Figure 84: Photo by Larry Ryan
Coach Varichak on his retirement from basketball with family members, wife Noka, and grand-daughters Vanessa and Lindsay Jacobson - 2008

My favorite custodian happened to be my father, George, who worked in the physical education building when we were both employed at Hibbing Community College. He was very fastidious and ruled that Activities Building with an iron hand. He had great help from two young men who are still on the staff today. Gary Lee was my basketball captain, graduated with a teaching degree, but decided to work full-time with the HCC custodial staff. On the other hand, Steve Ranniker, who became a full-time custodian, was chosen as the Cardinal Softball Coach and is doing a fine job with the assignment.

Richard W. Varichak

Upon moving to Hibbing High School, I discovered a trio of custodians who made coaching a little easier. Jim Jukich, who started at the high school and then transferred to the Lincoln Elementary School, was a go-getter who always anticipated our needs. Chuck Whitney, at the Lincoln, was our contact when we had to utilize the elementary facility for practices. John Uhrbom, at the high school, always put a couple of chairs on the gym floor behind one of the baskets for me and Doug Schmitz so we wouldn't have to undergo the uncomfortable seating in the stands.

Figure 85: Photo by Mike Miesbauer
Coach V. bids goodbye to the five seniors who were the last players in the Schmitz-Varichak era.
Chris Nyberg, Hailey Smith, Rachel Miesbauer, Coach Varichak, Kayle Barnhill, Katie McLaughlin

It was late in my coaching career that I had the luxury of having professional trainers at our games. From my Evant days to community college action, the coaches (meaning me), were responsible for tending to injuries, taping ankles and taking care of other assorted physical ailments. I received some training in my undergraduate years on how to attend to injuries but it was very superficial. I always shuddered when a player would go down with an injury. My thought was always to make sure I was doing the right thing and not hurt the athlete any more than they were already.

Then a talented married couple named Tom and Julie Lange came into our coaching life as a highly competent professional training

Fifty-Five Years on the Bench

team. They serviced both the college and the high school and we coaches now could breathe a sigh of relief. Both parents were also proud of their two daughter-athletes, Kate and Emily, who participated in volleyball and basketball. Kate was especially noted for her volleyball skills and after high school graduation went on to star at the University of Minnesota – Duluth. Tom and Julie were as different as night and day. Julie was extremely personable and outgoing. Tom was very quiet and reserved but between the two, they solved all our training woes. For a long time, I asked both of them to call me "Dick" as we were all professionals. But to this day, they still refer to me as "Mr. Varichak" and as parents; they were always supportive of my coaching experiences.

As I close out the final pages of the memory publication, I say goodbye to the five seniors of the 2011 Bluejacket girls' team. These young ladies are the last segment of the Schmitz-Varichak coaching era. So loads of luck to Christine Nyberg, Hailey Smith, Rachel Miesbauer, Katie McLaughlin and Kayla Barnhill, and hope you can bring another section crown home to Hibbing. You already have made our school and community the upper class of girls' basketball.

Figure 86: Photo by Al Higgins

Go, Go, Go!!!

Figure 87: Photo by Al Higgins
Give 'er tarpaper!!!

Figure 88: Photo by Al Higgins
What now?

Figure 89: Photo by Al Higgins
I don't believe it!

Figure 90: Photo by Al Higgins
No more fouls, Doug. Okay?

Figure 91: Photo by Al Higgins
That line? I can't cross *that* line!?

Figure 92: Photo by Al Higgins
Pick him up!

Figure 93: Photo by Al Higgins
C'mon Ref. Call it both ways!

The Final Buzzer

In preparing the contents for this book I found the task of including all my coaching experiences quite impossible. But – I was going to try! For fifty-five years I faced numerous situations, worked with thousands of athletes, and experienced a gamut of emotions – both exhilarating and disappointing.

I discovered a striking feature in the coaching world and that was the educational value which the profession reflects - not only for the athlete, but also for the coaching staff. I tried to bring this factor out with my periodic descriptions of how I changed my coaching philosophy and programs as I got older with added experience. These changes were also dependent on the caliber of competition, be it at an elementary, junior high, high school, or college level. This also includes the gender of the athlete because, as I pointed out in one of my chapters, there is a difference in program directions between male and female.

Collecting all these memories, assembled in the twenty-one chapters, was a pure labor of love. I have always enjoyed writing but this endeavor proved to me that the coaching profession was my lifetime calling. I am so indebted to the many athletes, parents, and colleagues who made this dream become a reality. I only hope my readers enjoy these memories as much as I enjoyed writing about them.

ILLUSTRATION CREDITS

1. Coaching Males & Females Guiding Principles
   Minnesota Prep Coach – Minnesota State High School Coaches Association, August 2009.
2. Relationships and Influence on Coaches Lives
   Rick Weegman, Sports Editor, Duluth News Tribune Newspaper Article, August 2002.
3. Informative Guide for Coaches in Establishing a Meaningful Relationship with Parents
   Minnesota Prep Coach – Minnesota State High School Coaches Association, August, 2007.

Richard Warren Varichak

Born May 4, 1931, to George and Mae Severson) Varichak in North Hibbing's General Hospital, the eldest of their four boys. Raised in the "Pigtown" section of Chisholm (lots of farm animals), he attended Roosevelt Elementary School, Chisholm Junior High School, and graduated from Chisholm High School with the class of 1949. He furthered his education at the University of Texas – Austin earning a Bachelor of Science degree in Education and a Master of Education degree (emphasis in Kinesiology).

Early in his elementary years he fell in love with sports and was an avid participant in several athletic activities. This led to varsity competition with the Bluestreaks, earning team letters in football, basketball, track, and baseball. He also was elected to captain both the basketball and baseball teams in his senior year.

An interest in writing developed in junior high which served him as the school's newspaper sports editor. Veda Ponikvar, the managing editor of Chisholm's Free Press newspaper liked his work with the school publication and hired him to handle her paper's sports section. She proved to be very instrumental in furthering his journalistic interest.

With the outbreak of the Korean War, he enlisted in the U.S. Navy in 1951 after spending a semester at the University of Minnesota-Duluth and a year at Hibbing Junior College. The first two years of active duty were spent in Japan – Korea where he served with Commander Naval Forces, Far East, the department which coordinated all ship movements in the Korean battle zones. In addition to military duties, he played and coached softball and basketball for the U.S. Navy teams and served as the sports editor of the base newspaper.

In his last duty station in Kingsville, Texas, he met Wynoka Carter, the love of his life. They were married on June 15, 1955 and after four children, fourteen grandchildren, and nine great-grandkids, are looking forward to fifty-eight years of marital bliss.

Upon his retirement from the Hibbing Community College where he served as a coach, faculty member, and Athletic Director, Dick was elected to the Minnesota Community College Hall of Fame as a former player, coach, and administrator.

He wrote his first book in 1999 entitled "Chisholm High School – 49ers – A 50 Year Trip Down Memory Lane." It includes a recap of all his eighty-six classmates and their lives after 50 years past graduation. This was his first "labor of love." He is currently working on a third book which reflects a multitude of whistle-blowing experiences enjoyed by sports officials.